Catholic Study Guides for Mary Fabyan Windeatt's

The Curé of Ars,
The Story of Saint John Vianney,
Patron Saint of Parish Priests

The Little Flower,
The Story of Saint Therese of the Child Jesus

Saint Hyacinth of Poland,
The Story of the Apostle of the North

Saint Louis de Montfort,
The Story of Our Lady's Slave

RACE for Heaven's Grade 7 Study Guides

Janet P. McKenzie

Biblio Resource Publications, Inc.
Bessemer, Michigan

The Curé of Ars Study Guide © 2003 by Janet P. McKenzie
The Little Flower Study Guide © 2001 by Janet P. McKenzie
St. Hyacinth Study Guide © 2001 by Janet P. McKenzie
St. Louis de Montfort Study Guide © 2003 by P. Janet McKenzie

Catholic Study Guides for Mary Fabyan Windeatt's Saints Grade 7 © 2007 by Janet P. McKenzie

Published by
Biblio Resource Publications, Inc.
108 ½ South Moore Street
Bessemer, MI 49911
info@BiblioResource.com
www.BiblioResource.com

ISBN 978-1-934185-09-4
Second printing 2015

A **R**ead **A**loud **C**urriculum **E**nrichment Product
www.RACEforHeaven.com

Cover photo of Obelisk and Basilica in St. Peters Square, Rome © iofoto - Fotolia.com

Special thanks to Julia Fogassy from Our Father's House for her editorial assistance

All quotations from the Windeatt biographies are excerpted from the edition published by Tan Books and Publisher, Inc. If using the original hardback version of these books, note that the text will be the same but the page numbers will vary from the Tan edition.

Printed in the United States of America

Table of Contents

Spiritual Read Aloud

Spiritual Reading

In *My Daily Bread, A Summary of the Spiritual Life* by Father Anthony Paone, S.J., Christ tells us,

> My Child, reading and reflecting are a great help to your spiritual life. My doctrine is explained in many books. . . . Some of these books are written simply, and some are very profound and learned. Choose those which will help you most toward a greater understanding and appreciation of My Truth. Do not read to impress others but rather to be impressed yourself. Read so that you may learn My way of thinking and of doing things.

In her book, *Saint Dominic, Preacher of the Rosary and Founder of the Dominican Order*, Mary Fabyan Windeatt quotes St. Dominic as saying, "A little good reading, much prayer and meditation...and God will do the rest." Father Peter-Thomas Rohrbach, O.C.D., states that spiritual reading is the "third essential asset for mediation" (after detachment and recollection). The great value he places on the habit of spiritual reading is expressed in his book *Conversation with Christ, An Introduction to Mental Prayer*:

> We live in a world devoid, in great part, of a Christian spirit, in an atmosphere and culture estranged from God. Living in such a non-theological environment makes it difficult for us to remain in contact with the person of Christ and the true purpose of life itself. We must, if we are to remain realistically attached to Christ, combat this atmosphere and surround ourselves with a new one. Constant spiritual reading fills our minds with Christ and His doctrine—it creates this new climate for us.
>
> In former ages, spiritual reading was not as essential for one's prayer life. People lived in a Christian world and culture which was reflected in their laws, customs, amusements, and their very outlook on life. This situation has radically altered in the last two hundred years, and men must now compensate for this deficit through other media, principally reading. And as the de-Christianization of our world continues, the necessity for spiritual reading simultaneously increases. We stand in need of something to bridge the gap between our pagan surroundings and our conversation with Christ—spiritual reading fills this need.
>
> There is today in our country an alarming decline in general reading of all types. It has been estimated that in 1955 an astonishing forty-eight percent of the American adult population reads *no books at all*, and only eighteen percent read from one to four books. The decline in reading is naturally reflected in religious reading as well. And, while the lack of secular reading will occasion a decrease in culture life, the decline in religious reading

will have repercussions of a more serious nature—severe detriment to one's spiritual life. Any serious attempt to better one's life spiritually should, therefore, include the resolution to engage in more spiritual reading.

If we confine our reading to non-Catholic books, magazines and newspapers, we almost automatically exclude ourselves from full development in our prayer life. The maxims and philosophy of life expressed in these avenues of communication slowly begin to seep into our lives until eventually they occupy a ruling position. We will not have surrounded ourselves with a new climate; rather, the non-Catholic climate will have engulfed us.

As this decry of the "de-Christianization of our world" was written in 1956, one can safely surmise that the necessity of cultivating the habit of spiritual reading can only have grown in the past several decades.

Spiritual Read Aloud

As supported above, spiritual reading is an essential element of every Christian's life. However, as demonstrated by the ancient practice within monasteries of spiritual read-aloud, this habit is a powerful tool for shared community growth in the spiritual life. For Catholic families, the practice of reading spiritual books aloud produces four desirable effects:

I.   It reinforces the habit of spiritual reading for each member of the family and allows each member to practice this habit regardless of age.

II. It reinforces the habit of spiritual conversation if the reading results in even a general discussion of the values and virtues being portrayed in the story.

III. It strengthens the family as the domestic Church where members exist to learn and live the Faith together for the support and enrichment of all family members.

IV. It allows the discussion and demonstration of the practical application of the Faith for all age levels.

The Habit of Spiritual Reading

As outlined above, establishing the habit of daily spiritual reading is essential to our spiritual growth. Through read-aloud, children can be taught at an early age that daily spiritual reading is a fun, rewarding exercise. Do make this time together pleasant by allowing the children to do crafts, draw, play quietly with puzzles, toys, etc. As long as their attention is not divided and they can participate in a discussion of the reading afterwards, allow quiet activity. One cannot expect children to sit piously with hands clasped prayerfully throughout the read-aloud session! As the children get older, encourage them to read other spiritual books, including the Bible, during a quiet time of their own. Model this habit by allowing them to observe your habit of daily spiritual reading as well. Although the family read-aloud sessions may be as long as thirty minutes, private spiritual reading times may be considerably shorter depending on the habits and temperament of each child.

The Habit of Spiritual Conversation

This habit, for many families, may begin with spiritual read-aloud. When each member of the family participates in a spiritual discussion of a religious book, the practice of discussing matters of faith and Christ-like living begins to form. If the formation of holy habits and imitation of the saints is the goal, these discussions will become common-place in the home as each member checks the others on their actions and words. As family members become more comfortable and open about spiritual matters, this practice will soon spread into other areas of their lives. Spiritual discussions with friends and other relatives will become more natural and in fact become important topics to be discussed. Sharing one's own spirituality and encouraging others to become more open about matters of faith will then become an integral pattern of living.

Strengthening the Domestic Church

As we read more about the saints and their lives and begin to share our faith more openly with others, we realize the importance of holy companionship—living with others who share our faith ideas and supporting each other in our attempts to become more like Christ. Families begin to grow together in their knowledge of the Catholic faith and become more willing to support each other throughout the ups and downs of community living. We begin to "bear one another's burdens with peace and harmony and unselfishness." Just as Christ has His Church to help bring salvation to all, we—as family members—have each other to provide mutual support and encouragement in our efforts to enter the narrow gate. Within our families, we can create the Catholic culture that is missing from our world's culture.

The Practical Application of the Faith for All Age Levels

When lives of the saints are read aloud in the family setting, all aged children can participate in a discussion of the imitation of the saint's virtues and holy habits. Each member can help others understand how to apply the lessons the saints teach us on a practical level. All family members can help choose a particular habit or virtue upon which to focus. A reward system can be established for virtuous behavior. A family "plan of attack" on non-virtuous habits and attitudes can be developed, implemented, checked, and revised. All members can be encouraged and taught to imitate Christ by the imitation of His saints.

Summary

Regular family read-loud sessions that center around the lives of the saints will benefit the family with an increased interest in reading—especially saintly literature, a growth in vocabulary, and an improved sense of family unity. Additionally, family members will be encouraged to develop the habit of spiritual reading on their own, will become more comfortable and experienced with spiritual conversation, and be able to apply the Truths of the Catholic faith, on a practical level, to all aspects of their lives—no matter what their age. The customs, habits, and attitudes of the family will more and more reflect those of the Catholic culture. Perseverance in this simple daily ritual will help to "bridge the gap between our pagan surroundings and our conversation with Christ."

When Mother Reads Aloud

When Mother reads aloud the past
Seems real as every day;
I hear the tramp of armies vast,
I see the spears and lances cast,
I join the thrilling fray;
Brave knights and ladies fair and proud
I meet when Mother reads aloud.

When Mother reads aloud, far lands
Seem very near and true;
I cross the desert's gleaming sands,
Or hunt the jungle's prowling bands,
Or sail the ocean blue;

Far heights, whose peaks the cold mists
   shroud,
I scale, when Mother reads aloud.

When Mother reads aloud I long
For noble deeds to do—
To help the right, redress the wrong,
It seems so easy to be strong, so simple
   to be true,
O, thick and fast the visions crowd
When Mother reads aloud.
—Anonymous

The Reading Mother

I had a mother who read to me
Sagas of pirates who scoured the sea,
Cutlasses clenched in their yellow teeth,
"Blackbirds" stowed in the hold beneath.

I had a mother who read me plays
Of ancient and gallant and golden days
Stories of Marmion and Ivanhoe,
Which every boy has a right to know.

I had a mother who read me tales
Of Gelert, the hound of the hills of
   Wales,

True to his trust till his tragic death,
Faithfulness blest with his final breath.

I had a mother who read me things
That wholesome life to the boy-heart
   brings—
Stories that stir with an upward touch,
O, that each mother of boys were such.

You may have tangible wealth untold,
Caskets of jewels and coffers of gold.
Richer than I you can never be—
I had a mother who read to me.
—Strickland Gullilan

How to Use These Study Guides

☀REVIEW☀ Vocabulary

Vocabulary words are listed at the beginning of each lesson. Words on the left are secular words and are given within the sentence structure. Allow students to guess the meaning of the italicized word before looking it up. This helps them to surmise the meaning from context, a skill that enhances reading comprehension and strengthens vocabulary. Vocabulary words listed in the right-hand column are Catholic vocabulary words. Help students identify any suffixes, prefixes or root words that might give clues to the word's meaning. To help with definitions and proper usage, use a dictionary. For Catholic vocabulary words, use a Catholic encyclopedia, dictionary, or catechism.

??? Comprehension Questions/Narration Prompts

These questions are appropriate for all age levels. They can be used several ways, depending on a student's ability. For students with difficulty in reading comprehension, read and briefly discuss these questions before reading the chapter. Discuss, too, the sub-title provided under each chapter heading in the study guide. The student will then know what content to watch for within the reading. If read afterward, the questions become a *test of,* rather than an *aid to,* comprehension. For students with adequate comprehension skills, use the questions for oral review after the reading to insure that important content has been absorbed.

Use these questions too as prompts for narration, which is simply the oral retelling of the story in the student's own words. It is a helpful tool to determine the level of each student's comprehension. All ages may benefit from the practice of narration. If done within a mixed age group, begin with the youngest students and have the older students add details to the already-related story.

Answers to comprehension questions are provided in the answer key.

Forming Opinions/Drawing Conclusions

More than relating events, these questions require the student to develop an opinion, or to uncover or discover material not expressly stated in the text. They are designed to develop thinking skills and do not usually require the use of any outside resources. Use this section with children grades five and up as the basis for discussion or as a writing assignment.

For Further Study

Appropriate for upper elementary through high school grades, this section requires the use of additional reference materials. These activities invite students to look more deeply at the historical events and people that shaped the times of each character. Topics in this section may be used for honing research skills, or for oral presentations and/or written reports.

✠ **Growing in Holiness**

These activities are different from the others in that they do not involve discussion or study as much as personal action and interior reflection. They can perhaps be considered "conversion activities" or "life lessons." By applying the spiritual lessons of the story to everyday life, the student is encouraged to develop habits in imitation of the saints—which is an imitation of Christ Himself. Remember to reinforce these activities with the student and to comment when they are observed in action.

Geography

The map provided with this study guide serves to orient the students with respect to space—*where* the action of the story is taking place—as well as to acquaint them with common geographical landmarks. Permission is hereby granted to photocopy maps for family or classroom use.

Timeline Work

The creation of a timeline allows students to place the story's events within a wider historical framework. Simple directions for making a timeline are included in the study guide. Students will need plain paper, colored markers, and a ruler.

✓ **Checking the Catechism**

For older students, these activities require a copy of the *Catechism of the Catholic Church* (*CCC*) or its *Compendium*. The references for the more concise *Compendium* appear in parentheses after the *CCC* citations. Older students can read aloud—and then discuss—the stated text paragraphs with an adult.

For younger students, use any grade-appropriate catechism to review the doctrines and terms as specified. An excellent activity book for multi-grades is Ignatius Press' *100 Activities Based on the Catechism of the Catholic Church* by Ellen Rossini. Discuss together how the specific topics from the catechism are illustrated in the thoughts and actions of the characters in the book.

Searching Scripture

Familiarize the student with the inspired Word of God by studying the biblical passages provided. Strengthen these exercises by occasionally requiring memorization of the verse(s). Stress that knowledge of Scripture is an important part of our faith education.

Note that Ms. Windeatt used the Douay-Rheims translation of the Bible, which was the translation in use in the United States until 1970 when it was replaced by the New American Bible in the *Lectionary of Mass*. The Douay-Rheims translation is taken from the Latin Vulgate, whereas the New American translation comes from the original languages of Hebrew, Aramaic or Greek (as the case may be for each specific book). For this reason, some of the books' names (as well as some of the Psalms' numbers) differ between these two translations. When these differences occur in the biblical citiations within this study guide, the New American references are given first with the Douay-Rheims references following in parentheses. All biblical references used in this study guide are from the New American translation.

✎ Test

The purpose of the test is to ensure that the student has comprehended the important events in each saint's life as well as the lessons the story intends to impart. An answer key is provided for these questions.

In addition to the test, many students will benefit from the completion of a book report. See RACE for Heaven's *Alternative Book Reports for Catholic Students* for additional information on book reports specifically geared toward saint biographies. Consider requiring each student to choose one of these reports or activities upon completion of the Windeatt biography.

Warning

These study guides are comprehensive. They contain activities for a variety of age levels and areas of study. Do **not** attempt to complete every activity for every lesson. Do only those exercises that are suitable for the needs of your current situation. Resist the impulse to be so thorough that the story line of the book is lost, and the read-aloud sessions become dreaded rather than anticipated. The activities are designed to enhance your reading—not to become the dictating tyrant of your read-aloud time together. If you are using these guides for young audiences, consider just using the comprehension and opinion questions as well as the "Growing in Holiness" section; use the maps as a geographical visual aid. Re-read the books to complete the more advanced activities in later years.

Another suggestion is to use the activities designed for older students in coordination with their history, geography, writing and/or religious curriculum. Each study guide could also be used as a complete unit study for hectic times when regular school may not be in session such as Advent, times of family stress (the birth of a new sibling, for example) or over the summer months. In reading the book and completing the activities, subjects such as religion, reading, writing, geography, and history can all be easily covered.

The most important rules to the successful use of these enrichment activities are

1. Be creative rather than obsessive.
2. Be flexible rather than overly structured.
3. Enjoy!

Study Guide for

The Curé of Ars, The Story of Saint John Vianney, Patron Saint of Parish Priests

The Curé of Ars

St. John Vianney, parish priest of Ars, France,
Overcame many obstacles just for a chance
To become God's priest
And then, when deceased,
A saint for His church despite the devil's advance.

The revolution in France affected John's course.
But prayer and hard work he did heartily endorse.
Called to be priest,
His prayers he increased.
His desire to save souls was his driving force.

With the help of his friends and heavenly aid,
He persevered 'til at last, John made the grade.
Ordained as a priest,
His troubles decreased.
Except hearing confessions—this right was delayed.

To Ars he was sent, a small town curé.
He fasted and preached against sin and decay.
They liked not this priest
Who battled the Beast.
The townsmen just wanted to party and play.

John suffered and sacrificed for every soul,
Spent many an hour in his confessional stole.
A priest who heard sin
Again and again,
The reading of hearts became his starring role.

For hours he'd listen; for solitude he'd long.
But wherever he went, the sinners would throng.
They loved this fine priest,
Who battled the Beast.
A model for priests, dedicated and strong.

Think what you can learn from this saint and his tale.
How you can apply it to help you prevail.
Then mold what you do
And boldly pursue
His pattern of holiness. Follow his trail.

Timeline of Events

Year	Event
1776-83	American Revolutionary War fought
1786	Jean-Marie Vianney born on May 8th in Dardilly, France
1789	French Revolution begins (to 1799); John Carroll named bishop of Baltimore; mutiny on the *Bounty* by British seamen
1791	Death of Wolfgang Amadeus Mozart
1799	Napoleon Bonaparte comes to power in France; poems of Samuel Coleridge and William Wordsworth popular
1802	France lifts ban on religious practices
1803	President Jefferson secures the Louisiana Purchase for the United States
1806	John Vianney begins his study for the priesthood in Ecully; makes a pilgrimage to the shrine of St. John Francis Regis in La Louvesc
1808	First typewriter made
1809	John is asked to report to the French army; Napoleon Bonaparte takes possession of the Papal States (until 1815); St. Elizabeth Seton establishes Sisters of Charity in Emmitsburg, Maryland
1811	John returns to Dardilly from hiding; two weeks later, his mother dies
1812	John attends the seminary in Verrieres
1815	John ordained a priest on August 13th but not given authority to hear confessions for several months; assigned as assistant pastor at Ecully; Battle of Waterloo; French monarchy re-established
1816	John Vianney and Pauline Jaricot meet for the first time
1817	Birth of Henry David Thoreau
1818	After death of Father Balley, John assigned to Ars as pastor (February 8); Mother Philippine Duchesne comes to the United States to establish the Society of the Sacred Heart
1824	Opening of *Providence*, a free school for girls; beginning of the nightly visits of the devil to Father John
1829	Braille alphabet first used in Paris, France
1830	Death of Benedicta Lardet, faithful teacher at *Providence*
1831	Samuel Francis Smith composes "My Country, Tis of Thee"
1837	Erection of a chapel in Ars dedicated to St. Philomena
1840	John Vianney suffers a near-fatal illness; he longs for solitude
1841	St. John Bosco ordained a priest
1845	Conversion of John Henry Newman; Irish famine begins (continues until 1850)
1852	John Vianney made a Canon for the cathedral in Belley
1853	Father John makes his third unsuccessful attempt to escape his duties in Ars
1858	Apparition in Lourdes, France, of Our Lady to Bernadette Soubirous
1859	Death of John Vianney in August
1861	Beginning of the United States Civil War (until 1865)
1869-70	First Vatican Council meets
1874	John Vianney declared venerable on October 30th; declared "Blessed" in 1905, and canonized by Pope Pius XI in 1925

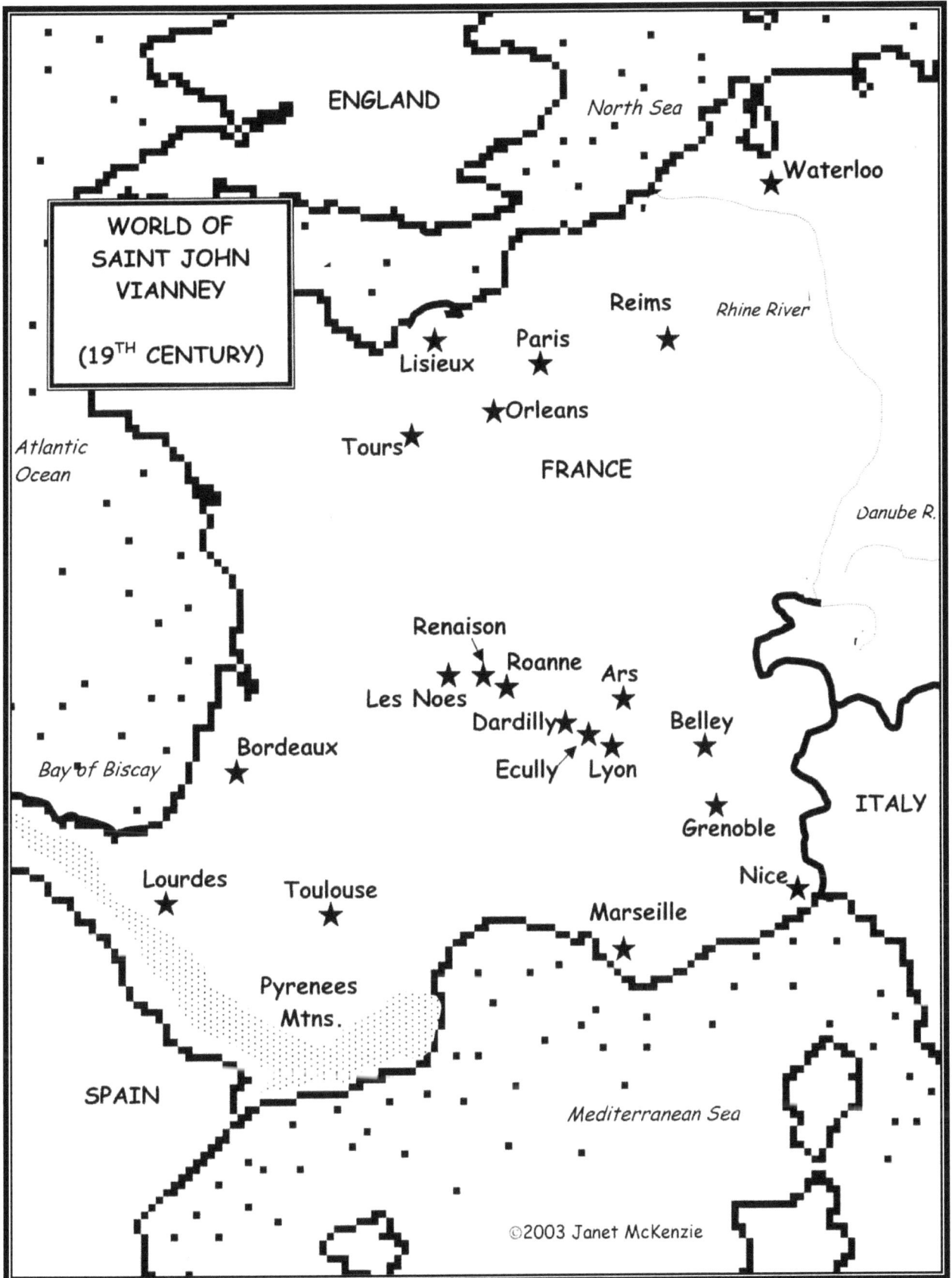

WORLD OF
SAINT JOHN
VIANNEY

(19TH CENTURY)

ENGLAND

North Sea

★ Waterloo

Atlantic
Ocean

Rhine River

★ Lisieux

Paris
★

Reims
★

★ Orleans

Tours ★

FRANCE

Danube R.

Renaison
★ Roanne
Les Noes ★ ★

Ars
★

Belley
★

Bordeaux
★

Dardilly ★
Ecully ★ ★ Lyon

ITALY

Bay of Biscay

Grenoble
★

Lourdes
★

Toulouse
★

Nice ★

Marseille
★

Pyrenees
Mtns.

SPAIN

Mediterranean Sea

©2003 Janet McKenzie

Chapters 1 and 2—In Which John Explains Life in France and Begins to Struggle with the Devil

✦REVIEW✦ Vocabulary

government had driven them into *exile*   *rectory*
Murmuring against God's will   *theology*

??? Comprehension Questions/Narration Prompts

1. According to John, what makes the struggle against the devil easier?
2. What did John do to help himself work more efficiently? Did it work?
3. John stated that there was a shortage of priests in France in 1802. Explain why.
4. Why did Father Balley refuse to accept John as a student for the priesthood? Who did John think was behind Father Balley's refusal?
5. Look on pages 8, 9, 14, and 19 to see how much formal schooling John had. What was he reading on his own to help prepare himself for the priesthood?

Forming Opinions/Drawing Conclusions

1. Why were so many religious activities—such as Mass and catechism class—done in secret? What it would feel like to attend Mass "as though bent on committing some great crime" (page 5)? How would this change your attitude toward Mass?
2. In what ways must we "struggle" to win Heaven? Who or what do we struggle against? What has God provided us as aids in this struggle?
3. Name three things that can be done to show what an honor and privilege it is to be present during the Holy Sacrifice of the Mass. If a "big name" star were coming to visit your church, would the church be full? How much excitement would there be? Jesus, our Savior, is present there at all times. Could you go visit him?

For Further Study

John speaks of the difficult times of the Church in France during the late 1700's. Research the political climate of France during the late 1700s. What was France's relationship with England, Austria, Spain, Sardinia, and Prussia as well as the Catholic Church? Include in your research the following: King Louis XVI, Napoleon Bonaparte, Pope Pius VI, Pope Pius VII, and the "Reign of Terror."

✝ Growing in Holiness

1. Memorize the last paragraph of Chapter 1 and use it as a morning offering. Recite it often throughout the day.
2. Outline a plan to ask the Blessed Virgin Mary for her help in a job you find difficult to do. List specifically what you want help with and how you plan to accomplish this through our Lady's help.

Chapters 3 and 4—In Which John Continues His Struggle to Become a Priest

---

✦REVIEW✦ Vocabulary

boxed my ears

My *woebegone* face

Major Seminary

grace of perseverance

⁇⁇ Comprehension Questions/Narration Prompts

1. How did John travel on his sixty-mile pilgrimage to La Louvesc?
2. Name four obstacles the devil used to discourage John from becoming a priest.
3. Why was John not excused from military duty as most seminarians were?
4. How did John come to be a deserter in the Army? What was his reaction to realizing that he was a deserter? What was his plan should the police come looking for him while he was a deserter?

💡 Forming Opinions/Drawing Conclusions

What did John mean when he confided to Father Balley that "only through pride could I have undertaken such an impossible venture" (page 24) as the priesthood? What virtues are demonstrated in this conversation?

✝ Growing in Holiness

God places great importance in obedience—doing the will of another before your own. Remember that He views this action as even more important than prayer and suffering. Try to receive as many graces as possible by being obedient.

🧭 Geography

Trace the map from page 3 of this study guide. Color these seas, oceans, and rivers blue: Atlantic, North, Mediterranean, Bay of Biscay, Rhine, and Danube. Also color the Pyrenees Mountains brown. (The map will be completed in Chapters 7 and 8.)

✓ Checking the Catechism

Older students may read text paragraphs 1830-45 (390) in the *Catechism of the Catholic Church (CCC)* regarding the fruits of the Holy Spirit. If desired, complete Activity #62, in *100 Activities Based on the Catechism of the Catholic Church (100 Activities)*. Younger students may reference this topic in their own catechisms.

📖 Searching Scripture

". . . an act of mortification can be tinged with pride, but never an act of obedience." (page 28) Read these Scripture texts: Samuel (1 Kings) 15:22, Psalm 40 (39):7-9, Micah (Micheas) 6:6-8, and Hebrews 10:5-7. Use these readings to reinforce your growth in holiness as discussed above.

Chapters 5 and 6–In Which Father Balley Continues to Inspire John

REVIEW Vocabulary

Vanities of the world
Ignorance and *vice* were flourishing

Brothers of Christian Doctrine
dispensation

??? Comprehension Questions/Narration Prompts

1. What was Father Balley's advice to John upon the death of John's mother?
2. What happened at the major seminary in Lyons to change John's plans for the priesthood? What was his new plan?
3. What was Father Balley's plan to enable John to continue his priestly studies?
4. For what priestly function did the authorities determine John to be unfit? Why?

Forming Opinions/Drawing Conclusions

1. We may not all be called to do great things, but we are all called to become holy. One way John's mother became holy was "by always doing little things well" (page 49). Give some examples of little things a mother may do well; name at least three things that you as a student and son/daughter may do well.
2. Why was Father Balley so insistent that John become a priest? What difference did it make whether John became a priest or a brother?

✝ Growing in Holiness

Each time you recite the rosary, add the following prayer after the Fatima prayer that concludes each decade: "God our Father, please send us holy priests."

Timeline Work

Taping sheets of plain paper end-to-end, make a timeline representing the years from 1776 through 1874. Let three inches equal 25 years. Mark on your timeline the dates and events from 1776 through 1812, using information from page 2 of this study guide.

✓ Checking the Catechism

Younger students should study the Sacrament of Holy Orders in their catechisms. Older students may read about this sacrament in the *CCC* in text paragraphs 1536-38, 1554, 1575-84, and 1590-1600 (322-336). If desired, complete Activity #46 in *100 Activities*, "The Fruits of the Holy Spirit." (Read too the two poems about priests found on page 20 of this study guide.)

Searching Scripture

Read Galations 5:16-26 on the fruits of the Holy Spirit and Isaiah (Isaias) 11:-2-3 on the gifts of the Holy Spirit.

Chapters 7 and 8–In Which Father John Begins His Priestly Life and Moves to Ars

✯✦✭✦✯ Vocabulary

Sublime words of Absolution
their own peasant *dialect*

Regina Coeli
curé

??? Comprehension Questions/Narration Prompts

1. What was Father John's first priestly assignment and how long was he there?
2. What did Father John say to make many people in Ars angry with him?
3. How did Father John describe true happiness as well as saintliness?
4. Why did the men of Ars not participate in the Corpus Christi procession?

Forming Opinions/Drawing Conclusions

1. Reflect on ways a specific priest has assisted you in becoming closer to Christ. You may wish to write him a thank-you note for his model of Christian service.
2. John Vianney refers to numerous sins the people of Ars habitually commit (page 75). Match these sins against a list of the Ten Commandments.
3. Why were the children's catechism classes one of Father John's first priorities?

For Further Study

Father John and Pauline Jaricot first met in Ars in 1816. Research the life of Venerable Pauline Jaricot, who established the Society for the Propagation of the Faith. You may wish to read Ms. Windeatt's biography of her. Present your research in an oral presentation or write a brief report.

✝ Growing in Holiness

". . . no one in Ars was in the habit of considering the real reason why he or she had been born . . ." (page 76). What would Father John see in your life that would give him cause to make this statement about you? Make a mental list of things you can change to better "know, love and serve God" in your daily thoughts and actions.

Geography

Complete the map started in Chapters 3 and 4 by labeling all cities red and the four countries green. On the map provided, cities are indicated with a star, and countries are in bold capitals. Notice the small sphere in which John Vianney lived.

✓ Checking the Catechism

Younger students may complete Activity #21 in *100 Activities Based on the Catechism of the Catholic Church* while older students read in the *CCC* text paragraphs 2590-97, 2683, and 2697-99 (534-577) on prayer.

Chapters 9 and 10–In Which John Converts the Souls of Ars and Starts a School

✖REVIEW✖ Vocabulary
Take a *deputation* to Lyons   *Vicar General*
Like a man *bereft* of his senses   *Sacred vessels*

??? Comprehension Questions/Narration Prompts
1. Why did Father John feel that the Vicar General was sending him away from Ars?
2. Why did Father name his new school *Providence*?
3. What did Father John think the nightly visitor was trying to steal?
4. According to Father John, the devil's appearance brought good news as his appearance was usually a sign of what?

Forming Opinions/Drawing Conclusions
1. Re-read Father's solution to ending his anxiety as found on the bottom of page 92 as well as the three paragraphs that follow this passage. Using the "I" of Father John to refer to yourself, state how to apply this spiritual lesson to your own life and how you can become an "Apostle of the Way of the Crosses." Be practical and state specific actions you can take or changes you need to make.
2. Pretend you are the devil attacking Father John. Explain your plan to torment John Vianney and why you are doing so. Conversely, pretend you are Father John. To whom do you pray as you battle against the devil? Explain your plan for dealing with the devil; be specific—what will you do and say?

✝ Growing in Holiness
The devil is real. When you feel his presence or temptations, invoke the name of Jesus, ask for Mary's intercession, or use holy water. St. Michael is also a powerful aid. Ask your guardian angel's help each night and throughout the day.

Timeline Work
Add the dates and events from 1815 through 1829 to your timeline.

✓ Checking the Catechism
Younger students may complete Activity #19 in *100 Activities* while older students participate in Activity #60. Both activities are on the commandments.

Searching Scripture
Father John assures Andrew that their guardian angels will look after them. Read Matthew 18:10.

Chapters 11 and 12–In Which John Becomes Known as a Confessor, and Miracles Begin to Occur at Ars

✗REVIEW✗ Vocabulary

I thought *wistfully*   *Confession*
spiritual as well as *temporal*   *Confessional*

??? Comprehension Questions/Narration Prompts

1. What was Father John's response when his friends exclaimed over the number of sinners he was converting?
2. With the exception of the Holy Sacrifice of the Mass, what prayer touches the heart of God in the most powerful way?
3. What did John Vianney feel was the greatest joy of the priesthood?
4. How did Father John explain the miracles that began to occur at Ars?

Forming Opinions/Drawing Conclusions

1. ". . . the outward form of a prayer does not matter so much as the spirit with which it is said . . ." (page 110). What does this mean? How can you apply this truth?
2. Why do you think St. John Vianney was made the patron saint of parish priests?
3. Who or what do you think is responsible for the miracles that occurred in Ars?

For Further Study

Research the life of St. John Francis Regis, who was born in France in 1597.

✝ Growing in Holiness

". . . the little ones could not rest until they had said 'thank you' to the friend who had helped them so wonderfully" (page 120). Find at least five people to say a special "thank you" to this week; write a thank-you letter to someone who has helped you in a special way. Frequently thank those in your immediate circle of family and friends—as well as God Himself for favors received.

✓ Checking the Catechism

". . . say just one *Hail Mary* each day for the conversion of our parish" (page 110). Complete Activity #70 in *100 Activities*, "The Hail Mary." Older students may read text paragraphs 2673-79 (562-563) in the *CCC*.

Searching Scripture

Father John spoke of the "extraordinary power which love has over the human heart" (page 114). Read 1 John 3:11-18, and 1 John 4:7-21.

Chapters 13 and 14—In Which John Craves Solitude and Leaves Ars for a Monastery

✎REVIEW✎ Vocabulary

great *calamity* had struck Ars
ached for *solitude*

sanctuary
assist at Mass

⁇⁇ Comprehension Questions/Narration Prompts

1. Why did Father John feel that prayers to St. Philomena would be answered?
2. What was Father John's own repeated prayer to St. Philomena?
3. About how many confessions did Father John hear each day at Ars?
4. Why did Father John wish to join a monastery?

💡 Forming Opinions/Drawing Conclusions

Why did Father John believe that he was empty-handed before God? (page 137) How did he wish to better prepare his soul? How well is your soul prepared?

📖 For Further Study

Give a summary of St. Philomena's life using the information contained in Chapter 13 as well as additional information obtained from outside sources. Include the role Pauline Jaricot played in St. Philomena's canonization.

✝ Growing in Holiness

John Vianney slept little and performed many penances for souls. Even his need for peace he gave to God: "Help me to take up my work again. . . . *Your* work . . . this very day!" (page 133). Can you honestly say that your work is God's work? Are you working to save not only your soul but also the souls of others? Remember Father Balley's advice: "The conversion of sinners begins with prayer and ends with penance" (page 61). Our Lady of Fatima reminded us of the need to pray and make sacrifices for sinners. Write down your spiritual plan to save a great many sinners.

✓ Checking the Catechism

". . . learn to know God better . . ." (page 142). Older students may read the following text paragraphs from the *CCC* on knowing God: 31-36, 50, 158, and 356 (3, 6-9, 66, and 90).

📖 Searching Scripture

". . . to learn to know God better. . . . to love Him . . . to serve Him . . ." (page 142). Read the following associated passages from Holy Scripture: Deuteronomy 10:12, Matthew 7:21, Luke 10:25-27, and John 14:21.

Chapters 15 and 16—In Which Father John Takes a Vacation and Returns to Ars

✥REVIEW✥Vocabulary

beseech you not to forsake us   *chaplain*
besieged with crowds of men and women   *Rector*

⁇⁇ Comprehension Questions/Narration Prompts

1. What did Father John and his friend John offer on the seven-hour trip to Dardilly?
2. What did Father John do before hearing confessions at the church in Dardilly?
3. What did Father John want for the pilgrims coming to Ars?
4. What special powers did God give to John Vianney?

Forming Opinions/Drawing Conclusions

1. What do you think the title of Chapter 15, "The Lost Week," means?
2. Describe Father John's "vacation."
3. "A priest must be willing to suffer" (page 165). Why? List several ways in which John Vianney suffered as a priest. In what other ways can priests suffer?
4. Why did the bishop want the Sisters of St. Joseph to take over *Providence*?

For Further Study

Research the various congregations of the Sisters of St. Joseph. When and where were they founded? What is their primary work?

✝ Growing in Holiness

"May the blessing of Almighty God—Father, Son, and Holy Spirit—descend upon you and remain with you forever." The practice of asking a priest for his blessing has sadly fallen out of use. Notice the people of Ars' pleas for Father John's blessing when he returns to Ars (pages 161-62). Remember to ask a priest for his blessing whenever possible. Has a priest blessed your house? Use blessed objects often, and always with care and reverence.

✓ Checking the Catechism

Older students can read about blessings in the *CCC* in text paragraphs 1671-72 (221, 351, 550-551).

📖 Searching Scripture

Read these passages from the Bible regarding blessings: Leviticus 9:22, Numbers 6:22-27, 1 Chronicles (1 Paralipomenon) 17:27, 2 Chronicles (2 Paralipomenon) 30:27, Mark 10:13-16, Luke 24:50-51, 2 Corinthians 13:13, and Ephesians 1:3.

Chapters 17 and 18—In Which John Accepts the Bishop's Ideas and Tries Again to Seek Solitude

---

✱REVIEW✱ Vocabulary

turning into a *miser*   *Trappist*
changed from a mournful *dirge*   *Breviary*

??? Comprehension Questions/Narration Prompts

1. Between the years 1847 and 1849, what happened to the schools Father John had started in Ars?
2. How did Father John raise money for the missions?
3. Why did Father John wish to go to the Marist house in La Neyliere?
4. How did Father Toccanier convince Father John to stay in Ars as the curé?

Forming Opinions/Drawing Conclusions

1. Explain why Father John might be grieved and "embarrassed" (page 175) by his title of "Canon"? What virtues does this illustrate?
2. What events helped convince Father John that his leaving Ars was God's will? How do you think he felt upon returning to Ars once again? How might you have felt?

For Further Study

Research the lives of St. Martin of Tours and St. Philip Neri. When and where did they live? Read enough of their lives to understand the circumstances in which the quotations attributed to each of them on page 191 were made.

✝ Growing in Holiness

"'I'm not using all my powers,' I decided. 'Somehow I feel that I could do much more for souls' . . ." (page 173) Search your own soul to ensure that you are using all of your God-given gifts for the greater glory of God.

✓ Checking the Catechism

To which of the commandments or virtues does each of these quotations pertain?

1. "I had allowed myself to become dangerously attached to my work with the little ones" (page 171).
2. ". . . the will of my Bishop. I had absolutely no right to question any official decisions which he should make" (page 171).
3. "But your Lordship, I haven't done anything. . . . God . . . His grace . . . the prayers and sacrifices of my friends . . ." (page 176).
4. "You made me promise to keep everything a secret, Father" (page 182).

Chapters 19 and 20—In Which John Continues to Save Souls until His Death

---

✖✿✌✿✡✖Vocabulary

typhoid fever   *Veni Creator*
showed no signs of *abating*   *curate*

??? Comprehension Questions/Narration Prompts

1. How did Father John ask Brother Babey to repay him for his advice?
2. What three reasons did Father John give for devotion to the Blessed Virgin?
3. At the age of 73, how many hours per day was Father John spending in the confessional?
4. What were some of the last concerns of Father John?

Forming Opinions/Drawing Conclusions

1. ". . . work for souls seemed at times beyond my strength. . . ." (page 193) How did Father Balley's advice to Father John on pages 50-51 continue to aid Father John in his last days? Notice how words of encouragement continue to sustain many years later.
2. What did Father John mean when he stated that, "This is the ending of all roads in the world . . . and the beginning" (page 209)?

✝ Growing in Holiness

"And I would save my soul by doing *my* duty, not that of anyone else, no matter how holy or how necessary it might be. . . . In short, I would prepare myself for eternity simply by . . . doing each day's . . . work as well as I could" (pages 192-93). Save souls by completing each task set before you each day with prompt, cheerful, and complete obedience.

Timeline Work

Add the events from 1830 through 1874 to complete your timeline.

Searching Scripture

Find relevant Bible references to the following quotations:

1. ". . . time given to helping a neighbor need never be taken from God, and . . . time given to God need never be taken from a neighbor" (page 193).
2. "All those who would *come to me!*" (page 193).
3. "God would be better pleased if I did without worldly honors and waited for the reward which He Himself had in store for me in Heaven" (page 194).
4. ". . . urged a devotion to the Blessed Mother" (page 198).
5. "My God!" I thought. "*My God!*" (page 209).

Book Summary Test for *The Curé of Ars*

Directions: Answer in complete sentences. If necessary, use the back of the page for additional writing space. 100 possible points, 20 points for each answer.

1. Name several obstacles that John Vianney had to overcome in order to be ordained a priest. How did he overcome these obstacles?

   _____

   _____

   _____

2. When John Vianney was first ordained a priest, what priestly function was he considered unfit to perform and why?

   _____

   _____

   _____

3. Describe St. John Vianney's encounters with the devil.

   _____

   _____

4. For what gift did the Curé of Ars become known? How many hours did he spend in the confessional each day? About how many confessions did he hear each month?

   _____

   _____

   _____

5. ". . . let me bring Him souls" (page 86). St. John Vianney sacrificed daily to save souls. What can you begin to do on a daily basis in imitation of St. John in order to save souls?

   _____

   _____

   _____

The Curé of Ars,
The Story of Saint John Vianney, Patron Saint of Parish Priests
Answer Key to Comprehension Questions

Chapters 1 and 2—In Which John Explains Life in France and Struggles with the Devil
1. According to John, the struggle against the temptations of the devil becomes easier when we remember to ask God to provide the grace to overcome these temptations.
2. Thirteen-year-old John helped himself work more efficiently by asking the Blessed Mother's help and reminding himself of her inspiration by carrying her statue with him when he worked. This system worked so well that his brother asked his secret and adopted it himself.
3. There was a shortage of priests in France in 1802 as so many had been murdered in the Church's persecution during the French Revolution.
4. Father Balley refused to accept John as a student for the priesthood as he did not feel John had a vocation to the priesthood. John felt the devil was behind Father Balley's refusal to accept him as a candidate to the priesthood.
5. To better prepare himself for the priesthood, John read the Gospels, the lives of the saints, and *The Imitation of Christ*.

Chapters 3 and 4—In Which John Continues His Struggle to Become a Priest
1. John walked the sixty miles from Ecully to his pilgrimage site of La Louvesc.
2. Four obstacles the devil used to discourage John from becoming a priest include the objections of John's father, Father Balley's objections, the difficulties John had with his schoolwork, and his call to military duty.
3. John was not excused from military duty even though he was a seminarian due to several factors: he lived at home and not at the seminary, his grades were very poor, and he was much older than the average seminarian.
4. John became an Army deserter when his detachment left without him. (He was visiting with Jesus in church and lost track of time.) His reaction to his "desertion" was humble dismay and concern for his family name. His plan, should the police search for him, was to hide in a hayloft.

Chapters 5 and 6—In Which Father Balley Continues to Inspire John
1. Upon the death of John's mother, Father Balley advised John to petition his mother in heaven for her continued assistance.
2. At the major seminary in Lyons, John was dismissed as a seminarian due to his poor academic progress; he decided to pursue a vocation as a brother with the Brothers of Christian Doctrine and give up his pursuit of the priesthood.
3. Father Balley planned to teach John himself in order to help him become a priest.
4. The authorities determined that while John was very holy, he was not very learned and would be unfit to hear confessions as he had not studied the required texts for this sacrament.

Chapters 7 and 8—In Which Father John Begins His Priestly Life and Moves to Ars
1. Father John's first priestly assignment was as assistant pastor in Ecully; he was there from the summer of 1815 until February 1818, when he was transferred to Ars.
2. Father John made many people in Ars angry with him when he preached on the evils that had taken root in many of the souls in Ars.
3. Father John described true happiness as that happiness which is to be found in becoming holy; a saint is a person emptied of worldliness and filled with God.
4. The men of Ars did not participate in the procession as they felt it would be advertising their piety to the world; it was acceptable for children, but they felt too conspicuous.

Chapters 9 and 10—In Which John Converts the Souls of Ars and Starts a School

1. Although the Vicar General stated that he was sending Father John away from Ars to improve Father John's health, Father John felt that it was more likely because he had not been successful enough in converting the souls of Ars.
2. Father John named his new school *Providence* as he was trusting God, by serving Him in the persons of little children, to look after all the school's needs. He felt we must always place our work and ourselves completely in His hands.
3. Father John thought that the nightly visitor was a thief trying to steal the beautiful new vestments that the viscount had given him.
4. Father John began to feel that the devil's appearance brought good news as his appearance was usually a sign that some great sinner would make his confession the next day.

Chapters 11 and 12—In Which John Becomes Known as a Confessor, and Miracles Begin to Occur at Ars

1. Father John's response to the number of converted sinners was to ask for prayers and sacrifices from the children, and to shrug off the power of his own prayers.
2. With the exception of the Holy Sacrifice of the Mass, the prayer that touches the heart of God in the most powerful way is the prayers and sacrifices of children—the young and innocent.
3. John Vianney felt that the greatest joy of the priesthood was that of leading a soul to realize that God is all love and that there is no earthly delight that can compare with learning to know Him and to do His Will.
4. Father John explained that the miracles that began to occur at Ars were not due to his intercession but to those of others'—Sts. John Francis Regis, John the Baptist, and Philomena.

Chapters 13 and 14—In Which John Craves Solitude and Leaves Ars for a Monastery

1. Father John felt that prayers to St. Philomena would be answered as she had appeared to him several times in visions; they had made an agreement—he would send those in need of healing to her and she, provided it was God's will, would cure the ill. She was to receive all the credit for the prayer intervention.
2. Father John's own repeated prayer to St. Philomena was for her to convince his bishop that it was time for Father John to retire from his priestly duties so he could spend more time on spiritual reflection.
3. Father John heard between one hundred and two hundred confessions each day at Ars.
4. Father John wanted to join a monastery so he could lead the life of a hermit and spend many hours each day in quiet contemplation and prayer.

Chapters 15 and 16—In Which John Takes a Vacation and Returns to Ars

1. Father John and his friend John offered ten rosaries on the seven-hour trip to Dardilly.
2. Before hearing confessions at the church in Dardilly, Father John obtained permission from the archbishop of Lyons; Father John was out of his home diocese and thus had no authority to hear confessions in Dardilly.
3. Father John wanted the pilgrims coming to Ars to find peace of mind and heart (page 163).
4. God gave John Vianney the gift of reading men's hearts—sensing their sins with knowledge of the past and future as it pertained to souls.

Chapters 17 and 18—In Which John Accepts the Bishop's Ideas and Tries Again to Seek Solitude

1. Between the years 1847 and 1849, the school for girls that Father John had started, *Providence*, was turned over to the Sisters of St. Joseph; the school he had started for boys was turned over to the Brothers of the Christian Family.
2. Father John raised money for the missions in two ways: he gathered donations from wealthy friends and charitable people, and he sold various items from his rectory to raise funds.

3. Father John wished to go to the Marist house in La Neyliere in order to have time to call to mind his own sins, weep over them, and prepare for heaven.
4. Father Toccanier convinced Father John to remain in Ars as the curé by reminding him of the examples set by St. Martin of Tours and St. Philip Neri.

Chapters 19 and 20—In Which John Continues to Save Souls until His Death

1. When asked how he could be repaid for his advice, Father John asked Brother Babey not to give him a gift or act of service, but to say a Hail Mary for him once in a while.
2. The three reasons Father John gave for devotion to the Blessed Virgin were that our Lady softens our hearts; that our prayers, when channeled through the Blessed Virgin, will assume a special perfume or attractiveness; and we should treat her as the doorkeeper of heaven—the giver of all mercy and grace.
3. At the age of 73, Father John was still spending around eighteen hours per day in the confessional.
4. Some of the last concerns of Father John were for the men working in the heat to keep his room cool, their families who were at constant prayer for him, and the pilgrims who had traveled so far to see him.

Answer Key to Book Summary Test

1. John overcame his father's objections by prayer (his own and his mother's), and Father Balley's objections by prayer as well as the intervention of his mother and brother-in-law. Hard work and perseverance overcame difficulties in his education. John's call to the military, and subsequent desertion of the army, were overcome by a general pardon for deserters.
2. Upon ordination, John was banned from hearing confessions. It was believed that he was not fit as he had not studied the required texts; he was not considered learned enough.
3. St. John endured nightly visits of the devil; the devil would shake his house and make loud noises, not allowing John to sleep. The worst visits usually preceded the confession of a great sinner the next day.
4. John's gift was that of reading men's hearts—sensing their sins with knowledge of the past and future as it pertained to souls. Spending eighteen hours per day in the confessional, he heard between one hundred and two hundred confessions per day—several thousand each month.
5. Answers will vary.

In Honor of God's Priests

The Beautiful Hands of a Priest

We need them in life's early morning. We need them again at its close;
We feel their warm clasp of friendship. We seek them when tasting life's woes.
At the altar each day we behold them, and the hands of a king on his throne
Are not equal to them in their greatness; no, their dignity stands all alone;

And when we are tempted and wander, to pathways of shame and of sin,
'Tis the hand of a priest 'twill absolve us—not just once, but again and again.
And when we are taking life's partner, other hands may prepare us a feast,
But the hand that will bless and unite us—'tis the beautiful hand of a priest.
God bless them and keep them all holy, for the Host which their fingers caress;
When can a poor sinner do better, than to ask Him to guide thee and bless?
When the hour of death comes upon us, may our courage and strength be increased,
By seeing raised o'er us in blessing—the beautiful hands of a priest.
(From an old prayer card, author unknown)

Thou Art a Priest Forever

To live in the midst of the world, without wishing its pleasures;
To be a member of each family, yet belonging to none;
To share all sufferings, to penetrate all secrets, to heal all wounds;
To go from men to God and offer Him their prayers;
To return from God to men to bring pardon and hope;
To have a heart of fire for charity and a heart of bronze for chastity,
To teach and to pardon, console and bless always.
What a glorious life! And it is yours, O Priest of Jesus Christ.
(From an old prayer card, author unknown)

Study Guide for

The Little Flower,
The Story of Saint Therese
of the Child Jesus

St. Therese

Even as a young child, Therese loved our God.
To pray and do penance for her was not odd.
Beginning at three,
She wanted to be
A Carmelite nun—this path she would trod.

Her four older sisters all taught her to be
So faithful and holy, especially Marie.
Her mother died young.
To her sisters she clung.
Papa called her his queen as she sat at his knee.

Therese got very sick—in fact almost died—
The Virgin's prayers for her set illness aside.
In short, Therese well,
Broke Satan's spell.
With a smile Mary cured her at the bedside.

Therese tried at fifteen a Carmel to enter.
Her father approved and tried to present her.
The answer was "No."
Therese then did go
To the pope; "Obey"—the advise that he lent her.

But then at last Bishop gave his consent.
So Therese entered Carmel—'twas just after Lent.
A Carmelite nun,
A spouse of the Son.
Her dream realized, she was now quite content.

She started to practice a new child-like way
Of showing her love to God more with each day.
Her life here was short
But it was the sort
That shows He is the potter, we are the clay.

Think what you can learn from this saint and her tale.
How you can apply it to help you prevail.
Then mold what you do
And boldly pursue
Her pattern of holiness. Follow her trail.

Timeline of Events of Therese Martin's Life

Year	Event
January 2, 1873	Birth of Marie Frances Therese Martin
January 4, 1873	Baptism of Therese
1875	Therese decides to become a religious
1876	At the age of three decides to refuse the Lord nothing
August 28, 1877	Death of Therese's mother, Zelie
Summer of 1878	Therese sees vision of her father's coming trials
Late 1879/early 1880	Therese's first confession
April 19, 1883	Pauline, Therese's sister, enters Carmel
May 13, 1883	Our Lady's smile; Therese recovers
May 1883	Beginning of spiritual trials
May 8, 1884	Therese's first Holy Communion
June 14, 1884	Therese receives the Sacrament of Confirmation
December 25, 1886	Feast of the Nativity – conversion experience of Therese
May 29, 1887	Therese receives her father's permission to enter Carmel
July 1887	Therese sees picture of Crucified Jesus and knows mission
September 1887	Therese's prayers and sacrifices save the soul of Pranzuni
November 20, 1887	Therese has an audience with Pope Leo XIII
January 1, 1888	Therese receives permission from bishop to enter Carmel
April 9, 1888	Therese's entry into Carmel
January 10, 1889	Therese receives habit
1890	Therese begins to meditate on the Suffering Servant and to study St. John of the Cross
September 8, 1890	Therese's religious Profession
January 1891	Therese named assistant to sacristan
February 1893	Therese composes her first poem
June 1893	Therese paints her first fresco
July 29, 1894	Death of Therese's father, Louis
January 1895	Therese begins writing her autobiography, Manuscript "A"
June 1895	Therese offers herself to Merciful Love
October 1895	Therese begins corresponding with Father Belliere, missionary
March 1895	Therese becomes assistant novice mistress
Holy Thursday, 1895	Therese has first sign of tuberculosis
July 3, 1896	Therese meets Father Roulland, missionary
September 1896	Therese writes Manuscript "B" of her autobiography
June 1897	Therese writes Manuscript "C" of her autobiography
August 19, 1897	Therese receives Holy Communion for the last time
September 30, 1897	Death of Therese after agony of two days
September 30, 1898	Therese's autobiography *The Story of a Soul* is published
June 9, 1914	Therese's Cause of Beatification introduced at Rome
April 29, 1923	Beatification of Therese Martin
May 17, 1925	Canonization of St. Therese, the Little Flower
October 19, 1997	St. Therese is declared Doctor of the Catholic Church

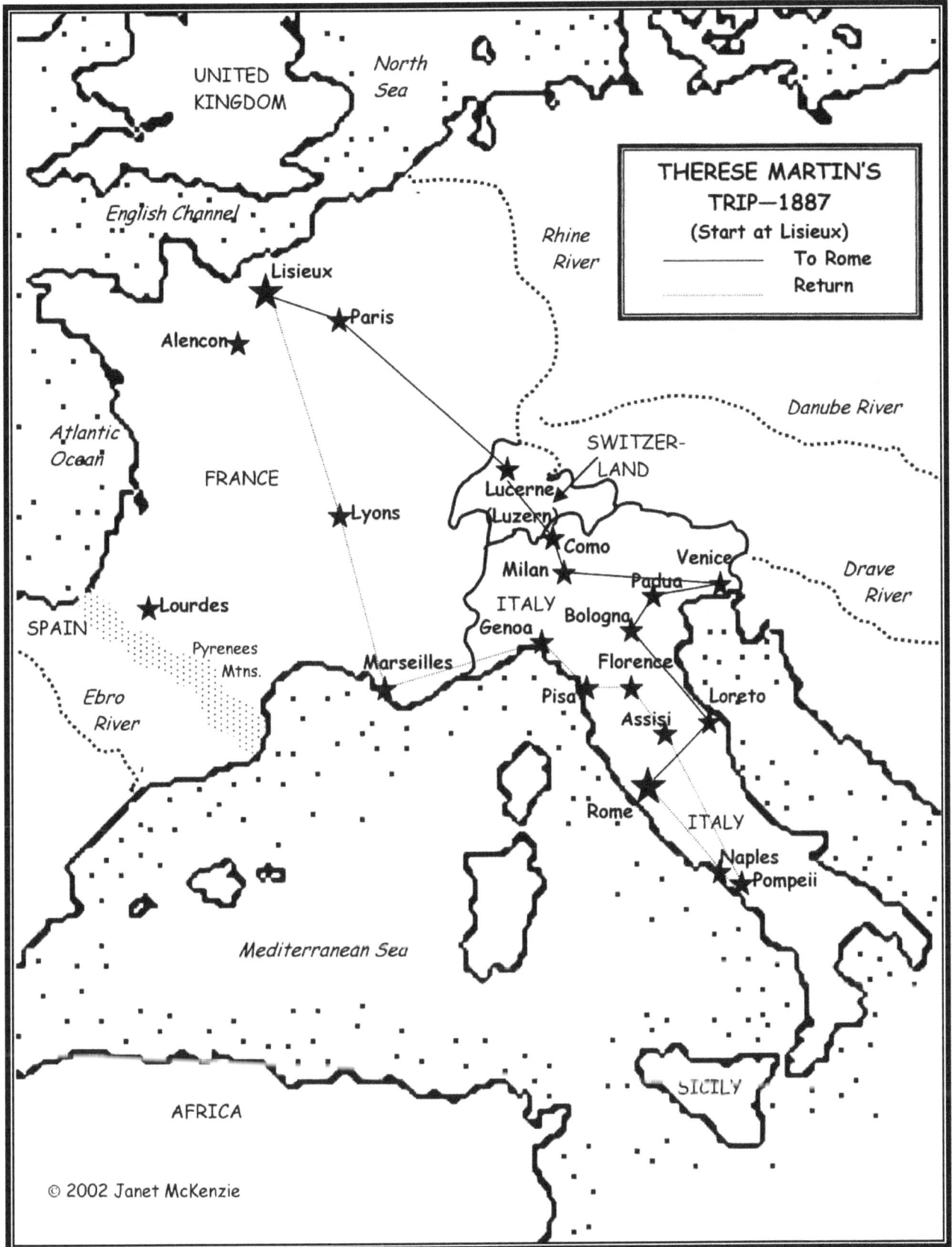

THERESE MARTIN'S
TRIP—1887
(Start at Lisieux)
—————— To Rome
.... Return

The Story of a Soul
Recommended Reading Schedule for Older Students

It is recommended that students who are twelve years old or beyond, read St. Therese's autobiography, *The Story of a Soul*, as an accompaniment to the Windeatt biography. The readings can be read on alternate days or after the chapter reading in the Windeatt biography. Ideally, parents and older students should read aloud together *The Story of a Soul*. If this is not possible, have the student keep a journal of quotations and insights of St. Therese. It could be divided into sections such as "The Little Way," "St. Therese on the Eucharist," "Love," "Suffering and Sacrifices," "Bible Passages," etc., or narrated by chapter.

A most edifying book on spiritual family life is *The Story of a Family, The Home of Saint Therese of Lisieux* by Father Stephane-Joseph Piat. Mothers especially will appreciate this book on the life of the Louis and Zelie Martin family.

(Both *The Story of a Soul* and *The Story of a Family* are available from Tan Books and Publishers, Inc.)

Chapter from the Windeatt Biography	Chapter from *The Story of a Soul*
Chapter 1	Foreword, Note and Prologue
Chapter 2	Chapter 1
Chapter 3	Chapter 2
Chapter 4	Chapter 3
Chapter 5	Chapter 4
Chapter 6	Chapter 5
Chapter 7	Chapter 6
Chapter 8	Chapter 7 (first half)
Chapter 9	Chapter 7 (second half)
Chapter 10	Chapter 8 (first half)
Chapter 11	Chapter 8 (second half)
Chapter 12	Chapter 10 (first half)
Chapter 13	Chapter 10 (second half)
Chapter 14	Chapter 11 (first half)
Chapter 15	Chapter 11 (second half)
Book Summary Exercises	Chapter 9 and Epilogue

Chapter 1—In Which Therese Is Born and Thrives

✝✝✝ Vocabulary

They were deeply *afflicted*

God heard the *fervent* prayers

Vincent de Paul

Visitation convent

??? Comprehension Questions/Narration Prompts

1. Why did some people think that the marriage of Therese's parents was a mistake?
2. Why did Therese's parents name all of their children—even the boys—"Marie"? Why was it important for them to have a boy?
3. What day was Therese born? What was her full name?
4. Why was Therese sent to live in the country with a nurse?

💡 Forming Opinions/Drawing Conclusions

Explain the attitude of Mr. and Mrs. Martin regarding the death of four out of their eight children. Why was their attitude different from those of their neighbors?

📖 For Further Study

1. List all the members of the Martin family, their birth dates, dates of death, and vocation in life. (In some editions of *The Story of a Soul* these are listed in the introductory materials or in the appendix. See answer key if assistance is needed.)
2. Junior-high school students (and older) should begin reading *The Story of a Soul* in conjunction with this biography. See the recommended reading schedule on page 24 of this study guide.

✝ Growing in Holiness

"Everyone marveled at the wonderful way in which Papa and Mama accepted these fresh trials. Death had called four times in twelve years, yet the Martin house was still a cheerful place" (page 4). Is your house a cheerful place? What immediate steps can you take to help it be a more cheerful place? Consider at least two positive actions that you can take toward this goal as well as at least two things that you can stop doing in order to help your house be full of Christian joy.

✓ Checking the Catechism

After the death of his two little sons, Therese's father stated, "The boys will pray for us. Just think! They went to God without one sin on their souls!" (page 3). Older students should read text paragraphs in the *Catechism of the Catholic Church* (*CCC*): 946-948, 950, 954-962, 1055, 1331, 1474-1477, and 2635 (194-195, 197, 211, and 554). Younger students may study the communion of saints and intercessory prayer in their own catechisms.

Chapter 2—In Which Therese Begins to Love Jesus

⟪REVIEW⟫ Vocabulary

grieving the Little Jesus   *pilgrimage*
owned a *chemist's* shop   *Lourdes*

⁇⁇ Comprehension Questions/Narration Prompts

1. By what pet name did Therese's father call her?
2. What did Mr. and Mrs. Martin do for a living?
3. At what age did Therese decide to become a nun?

Forming Opinions/Drawing Conclusions

1. What are some of Therese's faults? Give examples of each from the story.
2. Name three ways you can apply Therese's plan to become a saint to your life.

For Further Study

"A saint is a person who loves God and always says 'Yes' to Him" (page 16). Research the life of a saint of your choice. Find at least four instances in which this saint said "Yes" to God. How might his or her life been different if the answer in any of these instances would have been "No" or "Maybe later"?

Growing in Holiness

If you have a set of St. Therese sacrifice beads, use them to keep track of the sacrifices you make and good deeds you do each day. See how many times each day you can please the Little Jesus or say "Yes" to God.

Timeline Work

Taping sheets of plain paper end-to-end, make a timeline representing the years from 1873 through 1997. Let three inches equal 25 years. Mark on your timeline the dates and events from 1873 through 1884, using information from page 22 of this study guide.

✓ Checking the Catechism

Older students may read the following text paragraphs in the *CCC* on honoring the saints, relics, and images: 828, 1161, 1195, and 2683 (209, 240, 242, 264, 312, 429, and 564) while younger students reference these same topics in their own catechisms.

Searching Scripture

Read and memorize Psalm 134 (133).

Chapter 3—In Which Therese Loses Her Mother and Continues to Grow in the Good God's Grace

---

✴REVIEW✴ Vocabulary

spent many happy hours *angling*   *Carmelites*

daily *excursions*   *High Mass*

??? Comprehension Questions/Narration Prompts

1. After the death of her mother, Therese and her family move to Lisieux. State the name of their new home there as well as the meaning of this name.
2. Why were Carmelites "hidden from the world"? (page 25)
3. What effect did the priest's blessing have on Therese's rosary beads?

Forming Opinions/Drawing Conclusions

1. Describe the activities in the Martin house on Sunday, Therese's favorite day of the week. Compare and contrast with the activities in your house on this day.
2. Explain the meaning of the "merit of sacrifice" and the "merit of obedience" as used by Pauline on page 31.

For Further Study

1. Research the proper preparations to be made by the dying person and the family before the priest arrives to administer the Sacrament of Anointing of the Sick. The best resource for this may be an old prayer book.
2. Research the Carmelite order—its early history as well as the reforms initiated by St. Teresa of Avila and St. John of the Cross. What is its current status?

Growing in Holiness

Therese and her father made a habit of visiting Jesus in the tabernacle of the churches they would pass on their daily walks. Choose a time of day or a day of the week to visit Jesus as they did. Memorize the prayer Therese recited after her first confession (page 28) and recite it before the tabernacle—or in times of temptation: "My God, I give You my heart. May it please You to accept it, so that no creature can take possession of it but You alone, my good Jesus!"

✓ Checking the Catechism

Therese received the Sacrament of Penance when she was six years old: "I had been well instructed as to the meaning of Confession" (page 27). Read corresponding text paragraphs in the *CCC* including 1440-45, 1448-49, 1454, 1468-70 and 1485-98 (302-311). Younger students can review the procedure for a good confession in their catechisms.

Chapter 4—In Which Therese Attends School and Becomes Very Ill

---

⭐REVIEW⭐ Vocabulary

suffer their *taunts*   *novena*
sudden *calamity* struck   *Our Lady of Victories*

?? Comprehension Questions/Narration Prompts
1. How old was Therese when she began to attend school? Where did she attend?
2. What was the name Pauline received upon her admission to Carmel? What was the name Therese was to receive should she later be admitted?
3. Describe the spiritual battle that took place immediately before Therese's cure from her mysterious illness.

Forming Opinions/Drawing Conclusions
1. Give several possible meanings of the "vision" Therese had of her father.
2. Father Domin, the chaplain at the Benedictine convent, called Therese his "Little Doctor" (page 34). Why was this a prophetic statement?

For Further Study
1. "Two years later Leonie finished her studies at the Benedictine convent, and it was decided that I should take her place" (page 35). Research the religious order of St. Benedict. Construct an outline, or prepare an oral presentation with your findings.
2. "Suddenly, through God's Mercy, I felt a marvelous peace flood my soul" (page 39). Research the Mercy of God in Scripture as well as in the *CCC*. Do not exclude the Psalms, as they are rich in verses regarding His Mercy.

✝ Growing in Holiness
"Priests would be her (Pauline's) particular care. She would offer her life that God might bless the world with many good and holy priests" (page 36). As there are now fewer cloistered nuns to pray for priests, be sure to pray daily for "good and holy priests." After each decade of the rosary, add the following prayer: "God our Father, please send us holy priests."

📖 Searching Scripture
Read the story of Holy Week from Scripture; choose *one* of the following: Matthew 21:1-17 and 26:1—27:66, *or* Mark 11:1-19 and 14:1—15:47, *or* Luke 19:28-48 and 22:1—23:56, *or* John 12:12-19, 13:1-38, 18:1—19:42.

Chapter 5—In Which Therese Receives Her First Holy Communion and Confirmation, and Her Prayers for Peace Are Answered

---

✴REVIEW✴ Vocabulary

I was an *obstinate* child   *retreat*
enough to *banish* any sadness   *Child of Mary*

??? Comprehension Questions/Narration Prompts

1. How old was Therese when she received her first Holy Communion? How did she prepare? List the resolutions Therese made after her first Holy Communion.
2. How old was Therese when she received the Sacrament of Confirmation? For which gift did she feel a special need?
3. What was the second miracle Therese felt was performed in her life?

For Further Study

St. Therese divides her life before her admission to Carmel into three parts: before the death of her mother, from her mother's death until Christmas of 1886, and from Christmas of 1886 until her admission to Carmel in April 1888. Read the account of her "conversion" on Christmas Eve, 1886, in *The Story of a Soul,* Chapter V. Read text paragraphs 1264, 1426-33, and 1848 (165, 296-297, and 299-301) in the *CCC*. Christ continually calls us to conversion. How is He calling you?

✝ Growing in Holiness

". . . I had stumbled on the real meaning of meditation" (page 42). Set aside ten minutes each day to mediate. If necessary when beginning, use the verses of the Gospels to provide a starting point and to keep focused. Remember too the words of St. Philip Neri, "The best preparation for prayer is to read the lives of the saints. . . . And to pause whenever you feel your heart touched with devotion."

Timeline Work

Using the timeline provided on the next page, begin to keep track of your milestones in spiritual growth. Put the date of your birth, dates you received sacraments, converted your first sinner, and reached other spiritual goals you have set for yourself. Divide the timeline into spiritual phases, as did Therese to her life. Continue to add to this timeline. Use the timeline of Therese's life as a model.

✓ Checking the Catechism

Older students may read about grace in text paragraphs 1996-2000, 2003, and 2021-2024 (263, 266, 292, 341, 357, 359, and 422-425, in the *CCC*. Younger students may research this topic in their own catechisms, and then complete Activity #45 in *100 Activities*.

My Timeline of Spiritual Events

Year	Event

Chapter 6—In Which Therese's Soul Thirsts for Sinners and Grows in Grace

---

⟨REVIEW⟩ Vocabulary

he *fumed*   *conversion*
I felt very *dignified*   *works of mercy*

⁇⁇ Comprehension Questions/Narration Prompts

1. What prompted Therese's longing to suffer for the conversion of sinners?
2. Why did Therese join the Carmelites as opposed to a missionary order?
3. Therese delayed speaking to her father for several weeks about her decision to enter Carmel. Why?
4. Who were opposed to Therese's entrance into Carmel at the age of fourteen?

💡 Forming Opinions/Drawing Conclusions

Explain the difference Therese's conversion made in her life. How was she now leading a life much like the nuns in Carmel?

📖 For Further Study

Research the founding and history of the religious order of the Poor Clares. Who was their founder? What was their original purpose? Does the order still exist?

✝ Growing in Holiness

Until her entrance into Carmel, Therese wanted to "Pray for sinners. Look about and do good" (page 58). She felt that her first duty in her new life of charity was toward her own family (page 54). Think of ways you can bring love and kindness to your siblings and parents. Look for opportunities to imitate Therese in acts of charity within your family.

🗺 Geography

Trace the map on page 23 of this study guide. Color the seas blue: Atlantic, North, and Mediterranean as well as these rivers: Rhine, Danube, Ebro, and Drave. The remainder of the map will be completed in Chapter 7.

✓ Checking the Catechism

Older students may read text paragraphs 2214-20 (459) in the *CCC* regarding the duties of children. Younger students may review the fourth commandment in their own catechisms. If desired, complete Activity #63 in *100 Activities*.

📖 Searching Scripture

". . . Precious Blood falling to earth . . ." (page 53). Read John 19:31-37.

Chapter 7—In Which Therese Speaks to the Holy Father Regarding Her Entrance into Carmel

---

✭REVIEW✭ Vocabulary

were *heavy-hearted* on the trip home   *Jubilee*
coming down in *torrents*   *Noble Guards*

?? ??? Comprehension Questions/Narration Prompts

1. What question was settled in Paris at the church of Our Lady of Victories?
2. State the prayer Therese offered while in the Coliseum.
3. What was Pope Leo XIII's reaction to Therese's request to enter Carmel at the age of fifteen?

📖 For Further Study

Research the life and pontificate of Pope Leo XIII. On October 13, 1884, after celebrating Mass, Pope Leo XIII was given a vision of the future of the Church. In response to this vision, he composed a prayer to St. Michael the Archangel to be said at the end of each Mass celebrated anywhere in the Catholic Church.

✝ Growing in Holiness

If your family has not yet been consecrated to the Sacred Heart of Jesus—or if you have not yet made a personal consecration—consider doing so now. Many promises are attached to this devotion. For this consecration, a priest should bless a statue, picture, or icon of the Sacred Heart. After it is set in a place of honor, the consecration of the entire family is made using any number of prayers available in various prayer books. Renew this consecration annually or at Mass on the first Friday of each month.

🗺 Geography

Complete the map started in Chapter 6 by labeling the cities red and the countries green. On the map provided, cities are indicated with a star, and countries are in capital letters. Draw a solid line indicating the Martin's trip to Rome (from page 65) and a dotted line representing their trip home (page 76).

📖 Searching Scripture

"I drank in all I could, telling myself that when I was a Carmelite, with only a poor little cell and a patch of sky for scenery, I would remember the lakes, the wonderful mountains and forests through which we were now passing" (pages 64-65). Read Luke 2:19.

Chapter 8—In Which Therese Begins Her Life as a Carmelite Nun

---

✝REVIEW✝ Vocabulary

my desires are *rash*
Render thanks to the Saviour

Novice Mistress
Imitation of Christ

??? Comprehension Questions/Narration Prompts

1. How long did Therese's trip to Rome take?
2. Why did Mother Gonzago wait until after Easter before admitting Therese to Carmel?
3. Why did Therese wish to enter Carmel?
4. What duty was Therese given for exercise at Carmel?

Forming Opinions/Drawing Conclusions

Therese learned "a real lesson" (page 78) from the lamb given to her by her father. Re-state this lesson. How can you apply this lesson in your life? How is this lesson related to the required use of the word "our" instead of "my" in the cloister?

For Further Study

Research the lives of St. Teresa of Avila and St. John of the Cross. Write a brief report on each of their lives. Or prepare an oral presentation for your family.

Growing in Holiness

"I kept silent. A good religious is not expected to make excuses for herself, even when she is in the right" (page 82). Apply this to your life by not defending yourself against charges, righteous or not. Neither should you make excuses for your behavior or actions. This is especially difficult in a family setting, but remember the graces that will flow from this sacrifice. Offer these sacrifices for the conversion of a great many sinners.

✓ Checking the Catechism

Therese stated that she received consolation from her spiritual readings—*The Imitation of Christ* as well as the Carmelite readings of St. John of the Cross and St. Teresa of Avila. All three of these sources, as well as St. Therese herself, are quoted within the *CCC*. Refer to pages 741, 748, 750, and 751 for these quotations. Read these sources to see how they are used within the *CCC* to support our Faith.

Searching Scripture

Read and meditate on Matthew 5:48.

Chapter 9—In Which Therese Continues to Lead a Life of Sacrifice for the Salvation of Sinners

---

✦REVIEW✦ Vocabulary

a mild attack of *paralysis*   *mantle*
another kind of *raiment*   *Chapter Room*

??? Comprehension Questions/Narration Prompts

1. When did Therese receive the habit of the Carmelite order? How old was she?
2. What was Therese's special charge in the chapel?
3. Who delayed Therese's Profession of Solemn Vows?

For Further Study

1. Therese's dress for her Clothing Day was "made of white velvet and trimmed with Alencon lace" (page 88). After researching, write an essay on the making of lace as practiced by Therese's mother, who was known as a "Maker of Point d'Alencon." (See pages 34-36 of *The Story of a Family* by Father Piat for more details.)
2. What does this mean—"this last visit to the outside world, this last chance to embrace my beloved father" (page 89)?

✝ Growing in Holiness

Re-read Therese's description of her Little Way from page 88: "I gave myself and all my actions to our Lord . . ." Review too from page 95: ". . . no anxieties or trials of daily life are too small to be offered to God." Live the way of Therese—not by doing great things but by doing your daily duty with great love. Consider too St. Maria Faustina's quotation from her diary, *Divine Mercy in My Soul:* "I will not allow myself to be so absorbed in the whirlwind of work as to forget God" (Diary, 82).

✓ Checking the Catechism

1. Within this chapter, Therese mentions fourteen crosses or sacrifices. Try to find all of these. (Refer to the answer key if you need assistance.) Then review the fourteen Stations of the Cross—the sacrifices and sufferings of our Lord. See text paragraphs 1674 and 2669 (353) in the *CCC*. Younger students should read what their own catechisms teach about the Stations of the Cross.
2. Older students should read text paragraphs 901 and 2099-2100 (189 and 443) in the *CCC* which discusses the importance of offering our sacrifices to God.

📖 Searching Scripture

"When I was of assistance to her [Sister St. Peter], I was also of service to Him" (page 95). Read Matthew 25:31-40.

Chapter 10—In Which Therese Professes Her Vows and Lives Her Vocation

---

✖REVIEW✖ Vocabulary

influenza epidemic broke out
succeeded in painting a *fresco*

sacristan
oratory

??? Comprehension Questions/Narration Prompts

1. What doubt did Therese have the night before her Profession Day? What caused this doubt?
2. What two thoughts concerning her vocation consoled Therese after the death of her father?
3. What privilege came to Therese as a result of the influenza epidemic in 1891?

For Further Study

"You will see, Mother, that I shall make you change your mind about daily Communion after my death" (page 104). In 1905 Pope Pius X issued an encyclical entitled *Sacra Tridentina* which encourages daily Communion for all who are in the state of grace and approach the sacrament with the right intention. Find a copy of this encyclical and write a brief report on it. (It is readily available online and is not difficult reading.)

✝ Growing in Holiness

"He accepted my sufferings, offered in union with those of His Son on Calvary, and applied their merit to souls too lazy or indifferent to pray for themselves" (page 102). Our Lady of Fatima appeared on August 19, 1917—about twenty years after Therese made this statement—and implored, "Pray! Pray a great deal and make sacrifices for sinners, for many souls go to Hell for not having someone to pray and make sacrifices for them." With the shortage of cloistered nuns and monks to pray and make sacrifices, this statement is far more ominous today. Many souls are lost, as there is no one to pray and make sacrifices for them. Pray and make sacrifices each day for those souls who do not pray for themselves that they might be given the grace to convert and obtain heaven.

Timeline Work

Add the dates and events from 1886 through 1893 to your timeline of St. Therese's life.

Searching Scripture

Therese is tempted by the devil to give up her religious vocation. Read of Jesus' temptation in Matthew 4:1-11. We too must be on guard against his temptations.

Chapter 11—In Which Therese Begins to Write Her Autobiography

✖REVIEW✦ Vocabulary

conquered by your *vain* efforts   *canonized*
obeyed our Rule even in *trifles*   *cloistered order*

??? Comprehension Questions/Narration Prompts

1. In what method did Therese instruct the novices under her care?
2. One request that Therese made to our Lord on her Profession Day was for Leonie to be given a religious vocation and join the Visitation order. When was this petition granted?
3. Why was it difficult for Celine to enter Carmel?
4. Who ordered Therese to write down her childhood memories and why?
5. Who gave Therese the title of "The Little Flower"?

💡 Forming Opinions/Drawing Conclusions

Compare Therese's Little Way with the "Great Way" of other saints. What is your strategy to become a saint?

📖 For Further Study

1. Research the Visitation order—or Visitandines—as instituted by St. Jane Frances de Chantal. Compare and contrast this order with the Carmelite order.
2. Therese speaks of teaching the five novices in her spiritual care to become as little children. Read St. Maria Faustina Kowalska's words about spiritual childhood on pages 49-50 of this study guide.

✝ Growing in Holiness

Therese asked the Queen of Heaven to bless her new work—the writing of her childhood memories. Remember to ask this same spiritual assistance when you begin writing. Perhaps you would like to begin a journal of your own childhood memories and favors granted from God. Place the initials "J.M.J." at the top of each page you write to ask the blessing of Jesus, Mary, and Joseph in your work. This can make even your schoolwork an offering to the glory of God.

📖 Searching Scripture

In preparing to guide the souls of the novices, Therese states that on her own she cannot feed Jesus' children. Read in John 21:15-19 where Jesus commands Peter to feed His sheep. Note what is required of Peter.

Chapter 12—In Which Therese Continues to Guide Souls along the Path of Spiritual Childhood

---

⬥REVIEW⬥ Vocabulary

it was no *literary* masterpiece

as a *token* of her weakness

Foreign Missions

Sacristy

?⁇? Comprehension Questions/Narration Prompts

1. What offering did Therese, weak and little, make to the heavenly Father?
2. What is the only fear Therese had?
3. List three important events in Therese's life that took place in 1895.
4. State why Therese so loved to correspond with the priestly missionaries.

Forming Opinions/Drawing Conclusions

Why has Therese been given the title of "Patroness of the Missions" even though she was a cloistered nun? What can you do to evangelize the Good News?

✝ Growing in Holiness

"'When I think of all I have to acquire!' cried a novice one day. . . . 'You mean all that you have to lose,' [Therese] said. 'You are trying to climb a mountain, whereas God wishes you to *descend*'" (page 128). Sometimes we concentrate on obtaining holiness and acquiring virtue, when perhaps we should think of losing ourselves—our self-will, our worldliness. We need to fall as grains of wheat (John 12:24) and die to ourselves. We too can offer an oblation as Therese did. Compose an oblation of your own and pray it carefully each morning and in times of temptation. Perhaps you could tell God that each day you will offer less to Him, that each day by His holy love you wish to be made smaller until finally there is nothing left of you except holy emptiness that God can fill—or not—according to His Will.

📖 Searching Scripture

1. "Others achieve sanctity more quickly because they have learned to be humble" (page 127). Read and ponder Matthew 11:29.
2. "If you feel regret that all the flowers of your desires and of your good intentions fall to the ground without producing any fruit, offer to God this sacrifice of never being able to gather the fruit of your efforts. In an instant, at the hour of your death, He will cause the very best fruit to ripen on the tree of your souls." (page 129) Read these related Scripture passages: Psalm 1:1-3, Proverbs 1:31-33, Matthew 12:33-37, Luke 13:6-9 and John 12:24.

Chapter 13—In Which Therese Contracts Tuberculosis and Dreams of Being Called to Heaven Soon

---

✷REVIEW✷ Vocabulary

tuberculosis
fell *prey* to a bad cough

Repository
Lent

??? Comprehension Questions/Narration Prompts

1. How long does Therese feel she has yet to live?
2. What does Marie ask Therese to do in order to help Marie's willingness to suffer?
3. What doesTherese claim was one of her greatest sufferings at Carmel?

For Further Study

1. Chapter 9 or Manuscript "B" of Therese's autobiography, entitled "My Vocation Is Love," contains the portion written for Marie. It includes her account of the dream described in this chapter of Ms. Windeatt's biography. Be sure to read this chapter of *The Story of a Soul.*
2. Therese states that she made many acts of faith in the first year of her illness—more than in her whole previous life. Memorize an Act of Faith, or compose your own act of faith.
3. Research the life of Blessed Theophane Venard, a French priest who died in Vietnam on February 22, 1861, after being tortured and abused. He likened himself to "the spring flower which the Master of the garden gathers for His pleasure."[1] He was canonized by Pope John Paul II on June 19, 1988. How many other "Martyrs of Vietnam" were canonized on that day?

✝ Growing in Holiness

Therese stated that she made a novena to ask God for the favor of going to the Orient as a missionary. Pray a novena asking God for some favor you wish Him to grant. (Remember a novena is a prayer extended over a period of nine days and said for some special petition or occasion.)

✓ Checking the Catechism

Read text paragraph 826 in the *CCC*, a quotation of Therese's on the vocation of love. Read too other text paragraphs containing quotations of St. Therese of the Child Jesus and the Holy Face in the *CCC*: 127, 956, 1011, 2011, and 2558.

---

[1]Matthew, Margaret, and Stephen Bunson, *John Paul II's Book of Saints* (Huntington, Indiana: Our Sunday Visitor Inc., 1999), p. 64.

Chapter 14—In Which Therese and Her Sisters Prepare for the Death of Therese

---

✦REVIEW✦ Vocabulary

Prioress would send a *circular letter*   *godmother*
this little Sister is very *amiable*   *Prioress*

??? Comprehension Questions/Narration Prompts

1. What did Therese believe people need do to be truly free and happy?
2. For what did Marie hope when she placed the statue of the Blessed Virgin in Therese's room in the Infirmary?
3. By what way did Therese wish to lead souls?
4. What three predictions did Therese make before her death?

Forming Opinions/Drawing Conclusions

1. "Well, this little Sister is very amiable, but surely she has done nothing much since coming here" (page 144). These words spoken by one of the sisters at Carmel who knew Therese tell us that it is difficult to judge sanctity by outward appearances. What do you feel are some of the characteristics of sainthood?
2. Millions have read *The Story of a Soul*. How would it feel to know that countless souls not only would be brought into a closer relationship with God, but also might be saved for all eternity by your witness and example?

✝ Growing in Holiness

Re-read the first two paragraphs on page 148. Think of at least two rights or privileges that you have. Do not make the mistake of taking these "rights" for granted. Be aware that we all owe our "very existence to God's love." It is a mistake to get indignant or possessive of "rights" that are truly not ours.

✓ Checking the Catechism

1. Read about the role of godparents as outlined in text paragraph 1255 (259) in the *CCC*.
2. Older students may read corresponding text paragraphs 736, 1716-24, 1803-32 (or "In Brief" 1840-45), and 1999-2005 in the *CCC* on virtues and the Holy Spirit, especially the theological virtues of faith, hope, and charity (*Compendium* text paragraphs are 159, 371, and 377-388.)

📖 Searching Scripture

Find the passage from 1 Corinthians quoted by Therese. Create a poster or bookmark with this quotation using verses 4-7 and including verse 13.

Chapter 15—In Which Therese Continues Doing Good upon Earth

⟪REVIEW⟫ Vocabulary

let only His will be *manifest* in me   *Canticle of Canticles (Song of Songs)*
nothing escapes my *vigilance*   *Our Lady of Mount Carmel*

⁇⁇ Comprehension Questions/Narration Prompts

1. In what way did Therese wish to imitate Christ to the last?
2. What did Therese expect others to discover when they read her book?
3. What did Celine and Therese see as a sign of Therese's impending death? Why?

💡 Forming Opinions/Drawing Conclusions

On page 157, Therese gives a definition of holiness. Using a dictionary for the meaning of any words you do not understand, rephrase this definition of holiness into your own words. What can you do—or do differently—to attain holiness?

✝ Growing in Holiness

"Few people realize how furiously the Devil fights to drag souls to Hell, all during our life but most especially at the hour of our death" (page 159). Make an effort to mediate more deeply on the words of the Hail Mary the next time you pray them. Pray often that God will grant you the grace to obtain a happy death. Perhaps too you could begin praying each day at three o'clock in the afternoon—the hour of God's Mercy—for those souls who will die today that they too may attain heaven to love God for all eternity.

📅 Timeline Work

Add dates and events from 1894 through 1997 to complete the timeline on St. Therese's life.

✓ Checking the Catechism

Read text paragraph 1014 (206) of the *CCC*.

📖 Searching Scripture

1. Read the following Scripture passage: Luke 22:42. Why is it appropriate to read this verse now?
2. Read the Canticle of Canticles, also called the Song of Songs or sometimes the Song of Solomon. This parable of mutual love describes the union of Christ with His spouse which begins on earth and proceeds to all eternity. In this poetic book, the Lord is the lover and His people (especially perfect souls) are the beloved.

✎ Book Summary Test for *The Little Flower*

Directions: Answer in complete sentences. If necessary, use the back of the page for additional writing space. 100 possible points, 20 points for each answer.

1. List the members of the Martin family. How many of St. Therese's siblings were called to the religious life?

   _____

   _____

   _____

   _____

2. Describe Therese's journey into Carmel. List the steps she took to realize her vocation.

   _____

   _____

   _____

3. List Therese's duties and accomplishments as a Carmelite nun.

   _____

   _____

4. Relate how her autobiography came to be written. Describe each of the three sections, when they were written, and for whom they were written.

   _____

   _____

5. What factors helped Therese to become a saint? Why was she elevated to "Doctor of the Church" on October 19, 1997? How can you imitate her "Little Way?

   _____

   _____

The Little Flower, The Story of St. Therese of the Child Jesus
Answer Key to Comprehension Questions

Chapter 1—In Which Therese Is Born and Thrives
1. Some people thought that the marriage between Therese's parents was a mistake as they felt both were too holy to live in the world. A few people felt that Therese's parents should live their lives not as married people in the world but as religious people within a monastery.
2. Mr. and Mrs. Martin gave all of their children—even the boys—the first name of "Marie," which is French for "Mary." In this way, each child was consecrated to the Blessed Virgin. It was important for the Martins to have a boy as they wished to give a son to the priesthood to serve God.
3. Therese was born on Thursday, January 2, 1873—the youngest child of Louis and Zelie Martin. Her full name was Marie Frances Therese Martin.
4. Therese was sent to live in the country with a nurse, as her mother's ongoing battle with breast cancer prevented her from breastfeeding Therese. In addition, Therese was assured of receiving plenty of fresh air and sunshine there.

For Further Study
The members of Therese's family, in order of their birth, are as follows:
a. Louis Joseph Aloys Stanislas Martin—father of Therese; born August 22, 1823; asked for admission to the Switzerland monastery of the Great St. Bernard in September of 1845 but was denied as he knew no Latin; learned the trades of jeweler and watchmaker; married Zelie Guerin on July 13, 1858; died July 29, 1894 at the age of 70
b. Zelie-Marie Guerin—mother of Therese; born December 23, 1831; attempted admission to the Ladies of the Adoration in Alencon but was refused as the Superior felt it was not the will of God; in 1852 began to learn the art of lace-making; married Louis Martin on July 13, 1858; bore nine children; died at the age of 46 on August 28, 1877 of breast cancer
c. Marie-Louise Martin—sister of Therese; born February 22, 1860; joined the Carmelite order on October 15, 1886 as Sister Marie of the Sacred Heart; died January 19, 1940, at the age of 53
d. Marie-Pauline—sister of Therese; born September 7, 1861; became a Carmelite on October 2, 1882 as Sister Agnes of Jesus; served as Prioress from 1893-96 and from 1902-1951 except for an eighteen-month period between 1908-09; died July 28, 1951 at the age of 89
e. Marie-Leonie—sister of Therese; born June 3, 1863; entered Poor Clare convent on October 7, 1886, and stayed until December 1, 1886; entered Visitandine convent on July 16, 1887, returning home on January 6, 1888; second attempt at the Visitandine convent on June 24, 1893, where she stayed until July 20, 1895; definitively entered the Visitandine convent in Caen on January 28, 1899, as Sister Francoise-Therese; died there at the age of 78 on June 16, 1941
f. Marie-Helene—sister of Therese; born October 13, 1864; died at the age of five on February 22, 1870, after one day's illness
g. Marie-Joseph-Louis—brother of Therese; born September 20, 1866; died of erysipelas (acute inflammation of the skin) on February 14, 1867, at the age of five months
h. Marie Joseph-Jean Baptiste—brother of Therese; born December 19, 1867; died of bronchitis and an intestinal disorder on August 24, 1868, at the age of eight months
i. Marie-Celine—sister of Therese; born April 28, 1869; after caring for her father in his last illness, entered the Carmelite order on September 14, 1894, as Sister Genevieve of the Holy Face; died February 25, 1959, at the age of 89
j. Marie-Melanie-Therese, sister of Therese; born August 16, 1870; died of hunger at the hands of a nurse on October 8, 1870, at the age of two months
k. Marie-Francoise-Therese, born January 2, 1873; joined the Carmelite order on April 9, 1888 as Sister Therese of the Child Jesus and the Holy Face; died September 30, 1897 at the age of 24

Chapter 2—In Which Therese Begins to Love Jesus
1. Therese's father called Therese his "Little Queen."

2. Mr. Martin made his living as a watchmaker and jeweler; he quit this business near the end of 1870 in order to assist Mrs. Martin in her business as a "Maker of Point d'Alencon"—a craftswoman of fine Alencon lace. (See pages 34-36 of *The Story of a Family, The Home of Saint Therese of Lisieux* by Father Stephane-Joseph Piat, O.F.M. for more details or use an encyclopedia for pictures; see "lace.")
3. At the age of three Therese decided to become a nun; this was the same time that her older sister Pauline decided to pursue a religious vocation at Carmel.

Chapter 3—In Which Therese Loses Her Mother and Continues to Grow in the Good God's Grace

1. The Martin's new home in Lisieux was called *Les Buissonnets*, which is translated into English as "a wooded estate" or *The Elms*.
2. Mr. Martin explains that the Carmelite nuns are hidden from the world (or "cloistered") so that they can give all their time to loving God and bringing others to love Him.
3. The priest's blessing brought no visible effect to Therese's rosary beads, but Pauline explained that the prayers offered with the rosary would be more pleasing to God.

Chapter 4—In Which Therese Attends School and Becomes Very Ill

1. Although her sister Pauline (or her "little mother" as Therese called her) had taught Therese at home, she was almost nine before she attended school outside her home. It was then that she began her formal studies at the Benedictine convent as a day student.
2. Upon her admission to Carmel, Pauline received the name of "Sister Agnes of Jesus." Should Therese later be admitted, as was her current wish, she would be given the name of "Sister Therese of the Child Jesus."
3. Immediately before Therese's cure from her mysterious illness, she felt the devil battling for her soul. She tried to run from him but could not. Her sisters prayed desperately for her, especially Marie who implored our mother Mary to spare Therese's life. Suddenly, Therese felt at peace; the statue of the Blessed Virgin that was in the room became alive for her and smiled. Therese was cured.

Chapter 5—In Which Therese Receives Her First Holy Communion and Confirmation, and Her Prayers for Peace Are Answered

1. Therese received her first Holy Communion on May 8, 1883, at the age of eleven. She had begun her preparation four years earlier when Pauline had prepared Celine for first Holy Communion. In addition to Therese's instruction at the Benedictine convent, Marie also assisted each evening in her preparation. Pauline, now Sister Agnes, wrote numerous letters to Therese from the convent to assist in preparing Therese for Holy Communion. Pauline also composed a little notebook of prayers and devotions for Therese entitled, *Two Months and Nine Days of Preparation for My First Communion*. Therese attended a retreat at the convent for the entire week before the sacrament was to be given. In addition, Therese began to mediate for at least fifteen minutes each day. Therese made these resolutions after receiving her first Holy Communion: I will never give way to discouragement. I will say the *Memorare* every day. I will try to humble my pride. (Note that while Therese made her first confession at the age of six, she did not receive her first Holy Communion until five years later.)
2. Therese received Confirmation five weeks after her first Communion. She prayed for the gift of fortitude as she felt the joy of her first Communion slipping away.
3. The second miracle Therese felt was performed for her was in answer to her prayer for peace and a loss of her extreme self-consciousness. She was very sensitive and cried easily. She prayed that God would help her overcome this—to "grow up." On Christmas morning 1886, she felt her prayers were answered as she truly began to realize that all of God's children have been given a portion of the strength of the Child Jesus.

Chapter 6—In Which Therese's Soul Thirsts for Sinners and Grows in Grace

1. When a picture of the Crucifixion slipped out of Therese's prayer book showing one of the Savior's pierced hands, Therese was struck with an intense longing to suffer for the conver-

sion of sinners. This occurred a short time after her conversion experience around Christmas 1886.

2. Therese joined the Carmelites as opposed to a missionary order as she felt called to sacrifice for sinners by leading a life of prayer and penance.

3. Therese delayed speaking to her father for several weeks about her decision to enter Carmel as she felt he had been very generous already in giving up three other daughters to the cloistered life of a nun.

4. Many people were opposed to Therese entering Carmel at the age of fourteen or fifteen including her Uncle Isidore, her sister Marie, and Canon Delatroette (the priest in charge of the affairs of the Carmelite community of Lisieux).

Chapter 7—In Which Therese Speaks to the Holy Father Regarding her Entrance into Carmel

1. In Paris at the church of Our Lady of Victories, Therese had this question answered, "Had Our Lady really smiled on Therese and cured her when she was ten years old?." Our Lady let her know that she had indeed restored Therese to good health through the smile on the image of our Lady's statue; it was not mere imagination.

2. At the Coliseum, Therese asked God to let her be a martyr, "Dear Lord, please let me be a martyr, too!" (page 67).

3. Pope Leo XIII's reaction to Therese's request to enter Carmel at the age of fifteen was to tell her to do whatever the superiors in charge decided. He assured her that if it be God's will for her to enter, then she would.

Chapter 8—In Which Therese Begins Her Life as a Carmelite Nun

1. Therese and her family took a pilgrimage to Rome that lasted about a month.

2. Mother Gonzago wanted to wait until the difficult sacrifices and penances the Carmelites undertook during the season of Lent were completed before admitting Therese to Carmel.

3. Therese wished to enter Carmel to escape the trials and temptations of life in the world. However, her main goal was to save souls by giving her life, in union with Christ, for the redemption of sinners. She felt she should not seek any pleasure, even the most innocent, as these sacrifices were pleasing to God.

4. For exercise at Carmel, Therese was given the task of weeding the garden.

Chapter 9—In Which Therese Continues to Lead a Life of Sacrifice for the Salvation of Sinners

1. Therese received the habit of the Carmelite order, becoming a novice, on January 10, 1889. She was sixteen years old.

2. Therese's special charge in the chapel was the shrine of the Child Jesus—the statue of the Infant Jesus.

3. Canon Delatroette delayed Therese's Profession of Solemn Vows for eight months. The new date set was September 8, 1890, several months before her eighteenth birthday.

Checking the Catechism
The fourteen crosses or sacrifices mentioned by Therese in this chapter:
1. Her father's mild attack of paralysis
2. Her father's inability to visit Carmel
3. Her father's second attack of paralysis and subsequent illness
4. The cutting of Therese's beautiful curls on her Clothing Day
5. Her father's third attack of paralysis from which there was no recovery
6. His placement into an institution to be cared for by strangers
7. The humiliation of her father's mental state (Therese stated that he had joined his daughters in the Carmelite vocation of suffering for sinners.)
8. Therese's change of duty into the refectory
9. Therese's dealings with Sister St. Peter
10. Her early departure from the chapel each evening to assist Sister St. Peter
11. Therese's discomforts of weariness and cold

12. Her sacrifice of the lamp
13. Her sacrifice of the jar
14. Her disappointment in the delay of her Profession

Chapter 10—In Which Therese Professes Her Vows and Lives Her Vocation

1. The night before her Profession Day, the devil put an anxious fear in her mind, causing her to doubt her vocation as a professed religious at Carmel.
2. One thought concerning her vocation that Therese pondered after her father's death was the fact that she had come to Carmel to save souls—and especially to pray for priests. The second thought was her preference for sacrifice over all ecstasies—she preferred to serve God and imitate Him rather than have her senses full of Him.
3. As a result of the influenza epidemic in 1891, Therese was given the privilege of receiving the Eucharist daily.

Chapter 11—In Which Therese Begins to Write Her Autobiography

1. As Assistant Novice Mistress, Therese instructed the novices under her care in the Little Way to Heaven as developed by Therese herself.
2. Therese's Profession Day was on September 8, 1990. Leonie was accepted into the Visitation order in Caen several months after Therese began her work with the novices in February of 1893. Therefore, it was almost three years before God granted this petition of Therese's. (Note that Leonie entered the Visitation convent in Caen on June 24, 1893. She stayed at the Visitation convent until 1895; however, she returned in 1899 and stayed as a Visitandine until her death in 1941.)
3. Celine had misgivings about entering Carmel as she feared she would not be able to follow the rigorous Rule. There were also difficulties in obtaining permission for her entrance as three of her sisters were already professed nuns there.
4. In December of 1894, Therese's oldest sister Marie suggested to Pauline, the current Mother Prioress, that Therese write down her childhood memories. Marie thought that Therese could show what wonderful parents the Martins had as well as provide some spiritual insight that may be helpful to others.
5. Therese herself entitled her autobiography, *The Story of the Springtime of a Little White Flower*. She was remembering the white lily her father had picked and given her the night she spoke to him of her vocation and intention to enter Carmel. "Springtime" denotes her youth.

Chapter 12—In Which Therese Continues to Guide Souls along the Path of Spiritual Childhood

1. Therese, who had already abandoned her will to God and was following her Little Way of childlike trust, offered herself as a victim soul of His love.
2. The only fear Therese had was to keep her own will. She wanted God to take it; she would do whatever God decided for her.
3. Three important events in Therese's life that took place in 1895 include the following: a) the beginning of the writing of her autobiography b) the profession of her Act of Love and Oblation and c) the entrance of her cousin, Marie Guerin, into Carmel.
4. Therese was delighted to correspond with the priestly missionaries as she herself desired to become a priest and serve the Foreign Missions. The priesthood was close to her heart, and she was willing to suffer in any way to bring the Word of God to pagan lands. This was her way of bringing the Holy Faith to pagan lands; she could be a channel of grace for the labors of priests.

Chapter 13—In Which Therese Contracts Tuberculosis and Dreams of Being Called to Heaven Soon

1. Therese feels she has only a few months—a year or two at the most—yet to live. (Therese receives this premonition in the spring of 1896 and dies in September 1897—a year and a half later.)

2. As Marie perceives that Therese may have little time left to live, she asks Therese to write about her spirituality—just as she wrote about her childhood memories.
3. Therese claimed that one of her greatest sufferings while at Carmel was the coldness of her cell.

Chapter 14—In Which Therese and Her Sisters Prepare for the Death of Therese

1. Therese stated, "People cannot be free or happy until they have renounced all claims to freedom and happiness. Only when they have seen themselves as little children, depending on God's mercy for the very air they breathe, can they find peace" (page 148).
2. When she placed in the Infirmary the statue of the Blessed Virgin who had once smiled upon Therese, Marie hoped for a similar miracle—a cure for Therese.
3. Therese wished to lead souls by the way of spiritual childhood, the way of confidence and self-surrender. She liked to show souls the Little Way that had succeeded so perfectly with her (page 150).
4. Three predictions Therese made before her death include a) that there would be a *shower of roses* when she died b) that she would not only look down on us from heaven, but *come down* and c) that *some day everyone is going to love her.*

Chapter 15—In Which Therese Continues Doing Good upon Earth

1. Therese wished to imitate Christ by undergoing a death like his—one of agonizing sufferings.
2. Therese expected others to see God in a new light after reading her book. They would discover that He was not only their Judge but also their Father, and thousands of people would forget their fear of Him. They would joyfully set about achieving holiness by becoming little children.
3. Celine and Therese took the turtledove that appeared on the windowsill near Therese's bed as a sign of Therese's impending death. They recalled the words of Scripture in which the Lord calls His beloved (Song of Songs or Canticle of Canticles 2:10-14).

Answer Key to Book Summary Test

(Note that some of the following material is not from the Windeatt biography but has been added from other sources. Accept much more general information from the student for full credit and use the details of following information for enrichment purposes.)

1. St Therese of the Child Jesus had eight siblings, six sisters and two brothers. Her father was Louis Martin, and her mother was Zelie Martin. Her mother died when Therese was fours years old. Therese had four siblings that died at an early age—a sister Helene who died at the age of five, a brother Joseph who died when he was five months old, another brother Joseph who died at the age of eight months, and a sister Melanie-Therese who died at the age of two months. Therese also had four other older sisters—Marie, Pauline, Leonie, and Celine—all of whom joined religious orders. Four Martin sisters were nuns at the Carmelite convent in Lisieux—Marie, Pauline, Celine, and Therese—and Leonie joined the Visitation convent at Caen.
2. Therese's journey into Carmel began when she decided at the age of three, when Pauline entered Carmel, that she too would go to Carmel. On May 29, 1887, she received, at the age of fifteen, permission from her father to enter Carmel. On October 31, 1887, Therese unsuccessfully visited the bishop to obtain his permission as Canon Delatroette would not allow her admission due to her age—twenty-one was the usual age. Therese, Celine, and Mr. Martin then went to Rome. Therese asked permission of the Holy Father, Pope Leo XIII, to enter Carmel at the age of fifteen; he advised her to follow the decision of her superiors. On January 1, 1888, the bishop agreed to allow her entrance into Carmel. Therese was admitted to the Carmelite convent at Lisieux on April 9, 1888.
3. Therese's first duties as a Carmelite nun included household duties such as working in the linen room, sweeping the convent's stairs, weeding in the garden, and caring for the shrine

of the Infant Jesus in the chapel. Later she was given duty in the dining room and care of the elderly sister, Sister St. Peter. In the beginning of 1891 she was assigned assistant sacristan and assisted as nurse during the influenza epidemic later that year. She was given the duty in 1892 to paint religious frescos and draw holy cards, and also to try her hand at composing holy verses and poems. In September of this same year, she was assigned as second Portress, taking messages from visitors who came to the monastery on business. Near the end of 1893, Mother Agnes appointed her to be Assistant Novice Mistress, and in December of 1894, requested her to write her childhood memories. She was requested to write to Father Maurice Belliere, a seminarian and future missionary in October 1895. In May of 1896 Therese was given a second spiritual brother, Father Adolphe Roulland of the Foreign Missions. Therese was ordered to write to Marie of her vocation of love in September of 1896 and wrote the last part of her autobiography in June of 1897. She made no outstanding contributions to her community other than her example in living, and advising others to live her "Little Way."

4. Therese originally wrote her childhood memories ending with events of 1895; this took her one full year to complete, beginning early in 1894 at the request of Mother Agnes. The manuscript was given to Mother Agnes on the eve of her feast day, January 20, 1896. Next, in September 1896, she wrote a manuscript for Marie on her vocation of love, which Therese wrote in three days. In June 1897 Mother Agnes requested that she write another addition to her autobiography, which consisted of two rather lengthy chapters covering her life as a religious. Therese dedicated this section of her autobiography to Mother Gonzaga. In addition, Pauline recorded many of the sayings of Therese in the months before Therese's death. This material is a continuation of Therese's autobiography and makes up another entire book entitled *Therese of Lisieux, Her Last Conversations*. Note: Additional first account information regarding the life of St. Therese can be obtained by reading her letters. These have been published under various titles including the following:

   a. *Letters of Saint Therese of Lisieux: General Correspondence, 1877-1890* by John Clarke

   b. *Letters of Saint Therese of Lisieux: General Correspondence, 1890-1897* by John Clarke (out of print)

   c. *Collected Letters of Saint Therese of Lisieux* (edited by Abbe Combes, translated Frank Sheed—out of print but readily available)

   d. *Maurice and Therese: The Story of a Love, The Inspiring Letters Between Therese of Lisieux and a Struggling Young Priest* by Patrick Ahem, 1998 (This is the correspondence between Father Belliere and Therese that started in October of 1895, as mentioned on pages 124-126 of the Windeatt biography.)

5. Answers will vary.

St. Maria Faustina Kowalska, The Secretary of God's Mercy

These excerpts are taken from *Divine Mercy in My Soul*, the diary of St. Maria Faustina Kowalska, who was declared a saint on April 30, 2000. The words Jesus spoke to St. Faustina are in bold type.

On Spiritual Childhood

Here are a few words from a conversation I had with the Mother Directress (Mary Joseph) toward the end of my novitiate: 'Sister, let simplicity and humility be the characteristic traits of your soul. Go through life like a little child, always trusting, always full of simplicity and humility, content with everything, happy in every circumstance. There, where others fear, you will pass calmly along, thanks to this simplicity and humility. Remember this, Sister, for your whole life: as waters flow from the mountains down into the valleys, so, too, do God's graces flow only into humble souls.'

O my God, I understand well that You demand this spiritual childhood of me, because You are constantly asking it of me through your representatives. (Diary, 55)

When I started the Holy Hour, I wanted to immerse myself in the agony of Jesus in the Garden of Olives. Then I heard a voice in my soul: **Meditate on the mystery of the Incarnation.** And suddenly the Infant Jesus appeared before me; radiant with beauty He told me how much God is pleased with simplicity in a soul. **Although My greatness is beyond understanding, I commune only with those who are little. I demand of you a childlike spirit.**

I now see clearly how God acts through the confessor and how faithfully He keeps His promises. Two weeks ago, my confessor told me to reflect upon this spiritual childhood. It was somewhat difficult at first, but my confessor, disregarding my difficulties, told me to continue to reflect upon spiritual childhood. 'In practice, this spiritual childhood,' (he said,) 'should manifest itself in this way: a child does not worry about the past or the future, but makes use of the present moment. I want to emphasize that spiritual childlikeness in you, Sister, and I place great stress upon it.' I can see how God bows down to my confessor's wishes; He does not show Himself to me at this time as a Teacher in the fullness of His strength and human adulthood, but as a little Child. The God who is beyond all understanding stoops to me under the appearance of a little Child. (Diary, 332-333)

Today bring to Me the meek and humble souls and the souls of little children, and immerse them in My mercy. These souls most closely resemble My Heart. They strengthened Me during My bitter agony. I saw them as earthly Angels, who would keep vigil at My altars. I pour out upon them whole torrents of grace. Only the humble soul is able to receive My grace. I favor humble souls with My confidence.

Most Merciful Jesus, You Yourself have said, 'Learn from Me for I am meek and humble of heart.' Receive into the abode of Your Most Compassionate Heart all meek and humble souls and the souls of little children. These souls sent all heaven into ecstasy, and they are the heavenly Father's favorites. They are a sweet-smelling bouquet before the throne of God; God Himself takes delight in their fragrance. These souls have a permanent abode in Your Most Compassionate Heart, O Jesus, and they unceasingly sing out a hymn of love and mercy. (Diary, 1220-21— from the sixth day of the Novena to the Divine Mercy proscribed by Jesus to begin on Good Friday)

Today I heard these words: **My daughter, be always like a little child towards those who represent Me, otherwise you will not benefit from the graces I bestow on you through them.** (Diary, 1260)

(February 27, 1938) Today, I went to confession to Father Andrasz. I did as Jesus wanted. After confession, a surge of light filled my soul. Then I heard a voice: **Because you are a child, you shall remain close to My Heart. Your simplicity is more pleasing to Me than your mortifications.** (Diary, 1617)

On Love

Pure love is capable of great deeds, and it is not broken by difficulty or adversity. As it remains strong in the midst of great difficulties, so too it perseveres in the toilsome and drab life of each day. It knows that only one thing is needed to please God: to do even the smallest things out of great love—love, and always love.

Pure love never errs. Its light is strangely plentiful. It will not do anything that might displease God. It is ingenious at doing what is more pleasing to God, and no one will equal it. It is happy when it can empty itself and burn like a pure offering. The more it gives of itself, the happier it is. But also, no one can sense dangers from afar as can love; it knows how to unmask and also knows with whom it has to deal. (Diary, 140)

. . . **Tell all people, My daughter, that I am Love and Mercy itself. When a soul approaches Me with trust, I fill it with such an abundance of graces that it cannot contain them within itself, but radiates them to other souls.** (Diary, 1074)

Study Guide for

Saint Hyacinth of Poland,
The Story of the Apostle
of the North

St. Hyacinth

St. Dominic chose them and gave them a start.
He formed them and showed them to study by heart
The prayers they would need,
The rules they would heed,
But from them St. Dominic soon had to part.

St. Hyacinth and his three holy pals
Went back to Poland, with quite high morales.
They soon saw reward—
Souls saved for our Lord—
But then had to go into separate locales.

Purposefully, the apostles went their own ways.
Preaching the Gospel and singing His praise.
Devoted to Mary,
Their crosses to carry,
Converting the pagans with hearts all ablaze.

Hyacinth journeyed to Cracow and more.
He went many miles, the most of the four.
He taught them of God
And had them quite awed
By raisings and miracles, signs by the score.

Austrians, Germans, Fins, and some Russians,
Swedes, Czechs, Slavs, Poles, and plenty of Prussians.
He preached to the people,
Sometimes without steeple.
Far flocked the crowds for his holy discussions.

With faith and conviction in His Holy Name,
St. Hyacinth managed the pagans to tame.
Baptisms galore,
The rich and the poor,
One hundred-twenty thousand souls did he claim.

Think what you can learn from this saint and his tale.
How you can apply it to help you prevail.
Then mold what you do
And boldly pursue
His pattern of holiness. Follow his trail.

Timeline of Events

Year	Event
1155	Carmelite Order founded
1170	Birth of St. Dominic de Guzman
1174	"Leaning Tower" built at Pisa, Italy
1185	Birth of St. Hyacinth, son of the Count of Odrowatz
1189-1197	Third Crusade led by Richard the Lion-Hearted
1194-1260	Erection of Chartres Cathedral
1198	Peak of the medieval papacy
1202-1204	Fourth Crusade
1206-1227	Genghis Khan chief prince of Mongols
1209	St. Francis establishes the first rules for the Franciscans
1209-1227	Pope Innocent's crusade against the Albigensian heresy
1212	Children's Crusade
1214	Birth of Roger Bacon, Franciscan monk and English philosopher (died 1294)
1215	Magna Carta signed by King John of England, Fourth Lateran Council
1220	Hyacinth and his companions meet Dominic and join the Dominican order; Ceslaus becomes Prior in Prague; Herman becomes Prior in Friesach; Henry begins a monastery in Olmutz
1221	Death of St. Dominic
1224	Hyacinth becomes Prior of Holy Trinity Monastery in Cracow
1225	Birth of Thomas Aquinas
1227	Death of Batu Khan, leader of the Tartans
1230	Wenceslas, King of Bohemia (until 1253)
1231	Papal Inquisition
1238	Ceslaus calls a Provincial Chapter in Sandomierz
1240	Mangu Khan and Tartans invade Kiev
1241	Tartans leave Poland in April
1242	Death of Hyacinth's brother, Ceslaus
1245	Death of Herman and Henry, Hyacinth's original companions
1247	First Council of Lyons
1249-1250	University of Oxford founded; four colleges established at Paris University
1251	Simon Stock sees vision of our Lady and is given the Brown Scapular
1253	Canonization of St. Stanislaus
1256	Beginning of the Hundred Years' War between Venice and Genoa
1257	Death of Hyacinth at the age of 72 (St. Hyacinth was canonized by Pope Clement VIII in 1594)
1259	Kublai Khan rules Mongol Empire, Tartars return to Poland
1267	Aztecs arrive in Mexico
1268-1271	Three year vacancy in the papacy
1270	Marco Polo journeys to China
1274	Death of St. Thomas Aquinas; Second Council of Lyons
1275-1271	Marco Polo in the service of Kublai Khan
1276	Year of four popes

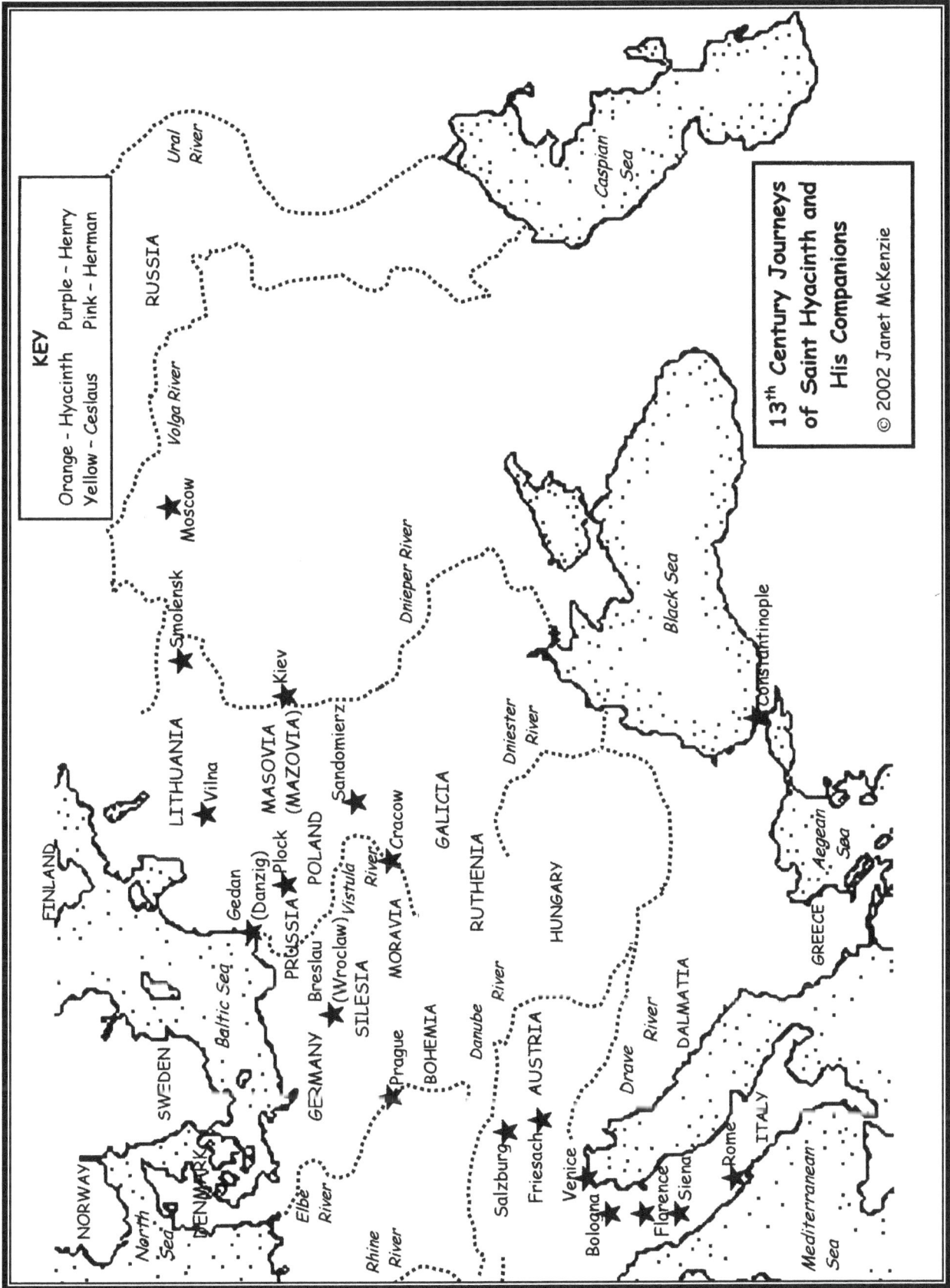

KEY

Orange – Hyacinth   Purple – Henry
Yellow – Ceslaus   Pink – Herman

13th Century Journeys
of Saint Hyacinth and
His Companions

© 2002 Janet McKenzie

RUSSIA

Ural River

Caspian Sea

Volga River

Moscow

Smolensk

Dnieper River

Kiev

Black Sea

Constantinople

LITHUANIA

Vilna

MASOVIA (MAZOVIA)

Sandomierz

GALICIA

Dniester River

Aegean Sea

FINLAND

Gedan (Danzig)

Plock

POLAND

Vistula River

Cracow

RUTHENIA

HUNGARY

GREECE

PRUSSIA

Breslau (Wroclaw)

SILESIA

MORAVIA

Baltic Sea

BOHEMIA

Danube River

AUSTRIA

DALMATIA

Drave River

SWEDEN

GERMANY

Prague

Salzburg

Friesach

Venice

Elbe River

Rome

ITALY

NORWAY

DENMARK

North Sea

Rhine River

Bologna

Florence

Siena

Mediterranean Sea

Poems to the Blessed Mother

To Our Lady

Lovely Lady dressed in blue—
Teach me how to pray!
God was just your little Boy,
Tell me what to say!
Did you lift Him up, sometimes,
Gently, on your knee?
Did you sing to Him the way
Mother does to me?
Did you hold His hand at night?
Did you ever try
Telling stories of the world?
O! And did He cry?

Do you really think He cares
If I tell Him things—
Little things that happen? And
Do the angel's wings
Make a noise? And can He hear
me if I speak low?
Does He understand me now?
Tell me—for you know!
Lovely Lady dressed in blue,
Teach me how to pray!
God was just your little Boy,
And you know the way.
—from *The Child on His Knees*

Mater Amabilis

How shall it be when we see her there,
With heavenlight radiant on her face
Making a glow of her shining hair,
Marking each fold of her garment's
grace?

Breathless in awe shall the angels listen
While we, the fallen, declare her ours
Though all the stars of the morning
glisten
Around her circlet of skyey flowers?

For only God and ourselves may claim
This loveliest, spotless, and sinless one
And call her "Mother"—O matchless
name!

Whose God and Creator is her Son.
Who shall have words for that breathless
hour
When death's dark slumber is past
awhile,
And heaven unfolds like a glowing
flower
That blooms forever in Mary's smile?

Mater Amabilis! Mother-my-own,
How shall I wait all the long years
through,
Unsated with beauty, in exile lone,
Searching the skies for a sight of you!
—Sister Sister Mary Jean Dorcy, O.P

To the Blessed Mother

Mother, I want to always be
Your child. Will you take care of me?
When God was just a little Boy
I know He gave you lots of joy;
And if He later made you sad,
I know that now He makes you glad.

And I believe if a child dies
That, when he gets to Paradise,
If you'll just touch God's hand and say,
"O *Please* don't sent that child away!"
God will say softly "Mother dear,
You can have all you ask for here!"
—from *The Child on His Knees*

Chapter 1–In Which Hyacinth Becomes an Apostle for Poland

✗REVIEW✗ Vocabulary

joyful *countenance*   *heresy*

in your *retinue*   *canon*

❓❓❓ Comprehension Questions/Narration Prompts

1. What miracle did Father Dominic perform in this chapter?
2. What did Bishop Ivo ask of Father Dominic? What was Father Dominic's reply?

📖 For Further Study

Research the life of St. Dominic, founder of the Dominican order, who lived from 1170-1221. Present your research in an oral presentation or a brief report.

✝ Growing in Holiness

The Bible cites many miracles that Jesus performed during his life on earth. We too have an opportunity to bear witness to a miracle each time we attend the Sacrifice of the Mass. Be mindful of the great miracle of the Eucharist the next time, and every time, you attend this Holy Sacrifice.

🗺 Geography

Trace the map from page 53 of this study guide. Color these seas blue: Mediterranean, Aegean, Black, Caspian, North, and Baltic as well as these rivers: Rhine, Danube, Dniester, Dnieper, Volga, Ural, Elbe, Drave, and Vistula. Each chapter we will chart the four apostles' travels. For this chapter, label the following: Rome, Prague, Bologna, Cracow, Poland, Prussia, Lithuania, and Germany. Label the cities red and the countries in green. On the map provided, rivers and seas are in Italics, cities are indicated with a star, and countries are in bold capitals. (Note that only the general locations of countries are indicated.)

✓ Checking the Catechism

Father Dominic performed a miracle in the Name of Jesus. Older students can read text paragraphs 430-435 (81-82) in the *Catechism of the Catholic Church* (*CCC*) on Jesus. If desired, complete Activity #5 in *100 Activities Based on the Catechism of the Catholic Church* (*100 Activities*). Younger students should review the Unity and Trinity of God as well as the Incarnation in their own catechisms.

📖 Searching Scripture

Read Mark 9:38-40, John 14:12-14, Acts 3:1-16, and Acts 9:32-35 to find out more about miracles that occurred in the name of Jesus.

Chapter 2–In Which St. Dominic Trains the Four Apostles

✖REVIEW✖ Vocabulary
He *rendered* it slowly   *Divine Providence*
in *deep* dejection   *Divine Office*

??? Comprehension Questions/Narration Prompts
1. What did the four apostles give up in order to join Father Dominic in his monastery? According to Father Dominic, how do men gain souls for Christ?
2. According to Hyacinth, what prayer does God always hear?
3. What are the two mottoes of the Dominicans?

💡 Forming Opinions/Drawing Conclusions
1. Express in your own words the two mottoes of the Dominican Order as explained on page 13. What can we do to live these mottoes out in our own lives?
2. What does it mean to strive to be a "worthier instrument of the Divine Will" (page 10)? On a practical level, how can you do this?

✝ Growing in Holiness
Reread Brother Henry's description of contemplation found on pages 13 and 14. Try this method of contemplation for fifteen minutes each morning for at least a week. St. Dominic believed that even very young children could obtain a knowledge and love of God. Remember too the difference between contemplation and mediation: contemplation is elevating the mind to God, whereas meditation is reflecting upon a spiritual theme. (See "Checking the Catechism" below for more information on these topics.)

🖼 Timeline Work
Taping sheets of plain paper end-to-end, make a timeline representing the years from 1155 through 1276. Let three inches equal 25 years. Mark on your timeline the dates and events from 1155 through 1215, using information from page 52 of this study guide.

✓ Checking the Catechism
Older students should read these text paragraphs in the *CCC*: 721, 2650-60 and 2705-24 (534-535, 557-577) on prayer. If desired, older students may complete Activity #99 in *100 Activities*. Younger students should review their own catechisms' sections on prayer.

📖 Searching Scripture
Read Matthew 19:21 on following Jesus.

Chapter 3–In Which Hyacinth Tells the History of the Church in Poland

✖REVIEW✖ Vocabulary

let the *ruse* pass   *Cistercian*

lent his *stalwart* frame   *Rule of St. Benedict*

??? Comprehension Questions/Narration Prompts

1. How far did the four apostles walk when they walked from Rome to Cracow?
2. What is the secret of Herman's spiritual progress?
3. What did Father Dominic predict would happen on August 6, 1221?
4. Why did Father Dominic not go as a missionary to Asia or Poland?

Forming Opinions/Drawing Conclusions

1. Name several modern-day people from Poland who may fulfill the prophecy of Father Dominic regarding people of Poland who will rise up to love and serve God (page 30).
2. Compare and contrast the prayers and purposes of the Divine Office (Liturgy of the Hours) and the Mass. Consider what prayers make up these liturgies, who participates, and the desired effect of the prayers.

For Further Study

Adopt a country that you feel needs to be evangelized and become a spiritual missionary to this country by praying for it daily. Research this country to find out when (if ever) the Christian faith was brought there and what percentage of the current population is now Christian. Have persecutions of Christians occurred there? Just as Father Dominic longed to go to Poland to be a missionary and never made it, we may never be traveling missionaries. But we may still obtain grace and support others' efforts to spread the Faith through our prayers.

Growing in Holiness

The various hours of Divine Office are explained in this chapter. There are now five hours: Office of the Readings (formerly Matins), Morning Prayer (formerly Lauds), Daytime Prayer (formerly Terce—9 a.m., Sext—noon, None—3 p.m.), Evening Prayer (formerly Vespers), and Night Prayer (formerly Compline). Say a short prayer today at each of these times, or choose a Psalm to read for each hour.

Geography

Appropriately label the following general locations on your map: Italy, Greece, Bohemia, and Russia.

Chapter 4–In Which the Four Apostles Leave St. Dominic

✖✖✖✖✖ Vocabulary

welcome would be *accorded* there   *postulants*
found themselves *besieged* by . . . crowds   *Prior*

??? Comprehension Questions/Narration Prompts

1. When Father Dominic sent the four apostles on their way, whom did he place in charge?
2. Why did the four friars stay at monasteries whenever possible when traveling?

💡 Forming Opinions/Drawing Conclusions

"For a zealous and holy priest has an enormous influence over others" (page 36). By what actions or words do priests get opportunities to influence other people? Listen closely when a priest speaks. Remember to pray often for an increase of holy priests.

📖 For Further Study

Read again on pages 32-35 how Father Dominic felt upon parting company with his young apostles. Then read Jesus' prayer for his disciples and believers before his death in John 17:9-26. Compare and contrast these two events.

✝ Growing in Holiness

Reread Brother Henry's discussion of prayer on pages 33 and 34. Remember to visit Jesus in the Blessed Sacrament to offer your prayers for someone you know or for the Holy Souls in Purgatory. Try to make small aspirations or ejaculations throughout the day: "I love you, Jesus!" "Jesus, Mary and Joseph, pray for us!" "Holy Spirit, inspire me!" "Jesus, I trust in you!" Short prayers are no less powerful than ones of longer lengths. Pray often.

🗺 Geography

Appropriately label (bold capitals for countries, etc.) the following destinations of St. Hyacinth on your map: Siena, Florence, Venice, Salzburg, Friesach, and Austria. Draw a dashed black line from Rome to Friesach to illustrate the travels of Hyacinth and his three companions.

📖 Searching Scripture

Hyacinth traces a path from humility to holiness to child-like trust. Read Matthew 18:3, Matthew 19:14, and 1 Corinthians 14:20.

Chapter 5–In Which the Preaching and Sacrifices of the Four Apostles Begin to Be Rewarded

✦REVIEW✦ Vocabulary

who *dispensed* the Sacraments   *Archbishop*
face was so *solemn*   *cathedral*

??? Comprehension Questions/Narration Prompts

1. What made Hyacinth marvel "at the wonderful ways of God" (page 45)?
2. What does he claim is "the most wonderful medicine in the world"?
3. What are the twin tools we are to use to build our "ladder to Heaven" (page 48)?

Forming Opinions/Drawing Conclusions

Explain how the daily life of the Friars Preachers (Dominican priests) varied from the life of the Franciscan friars or the Benedictine priests.

For Further Study

1. Hyacinth spoke of Mary as called by God. Research other Biblical characters who were called by God and how God called them—Moses, David, the Old Testament prophets, St. Peter, etc. Reflect on how God is calling you.
2. Read the poems about Mary from page 54 of this study guide. Perhaps you would like to compose a poem of your own to the Blessed Mother.

✝ Growing in Holiness

Memorize the prayer composed by Brother Herman on page 48: "Sweetest Jesus, grant that I may praise with my mouth, cherish with my heart, and honor by my actions Thy most loving Mother and mine." Make this prayer a morning offering or pray it in times of temptation.

Timeline Work

Add the dates and events from 1220 through 1231 to your timeline.

✓ Checking the Catechism

Older students should read about the Blessed Virgin from the *CCC* in text paragraphs 971, 2146, and 2673-79 (95-100, 142, 196-199, 429, 546-547, and 562-563). If desired, complete Activity #23 in *100 Activities*. Younger students may study this topic from their own catechisms.

Chapter 6—In Which Hyacinth Reaches Cracow Alone

✴REVIEW✴ Vocabulary

a slow and *excruciating* death   *secular clergy*
to *exhort* the people   *Norbertine*

??? Comprehension Questions/Narration Prompts

1. To what did Hyacinth attribute Father Dominic's success as a preacher?
2. To what countries does Hyacinth prophesize that he and Ceslaus would go as missionaries?
3. How does Hyacinth feel we can experience true peace in this world?
4. What is the purpose of establishing a convent of nuns affiliated with the four apostles' work?

Forming Opinions/Drawing Conclusions

In this chapter, both Hyacinth and Brother Henry speak of the importance of leaning on God and learning His Holy Will for each of us. Reread these passages in this chapter and summarize their lesson. What can your do to apply this lesson to your own daily life?

For Further Study

Hyacinth quoted Jesus and Holy Scripture when he stated, "Not my will but Thine be done!" Find this quote in the Gospels. Cite the chapter and verse where this quotation may be found. Compare the occasion of Christ's use of these words with Hyacinth's.

✝ Growing in Holiness

Remember Ceslaus' cheerful obedience to the new assignment given him by Hyacinth. Try to keep the fourth commandment as Ceslaus did—by setting his will aside in obedience to his superior. Be cheerful in your obedience to parents and others in authority over you.

Geography

Appropriately label the following on your map of the four apostles' travels: Silesia, Ruthenia, and Moravia. Draw dashed lines from Friesach to illustrate the following: In yellow to Prague for Ceslaus, in purple to Moravia for Henry, and in orange to Cracow to continue Hyacinth's journey. Highlight Friesach in pink to illustrate where Herman stayed.

Chapter 7–In Which Hyacinth Establishes a Monastery in Cracow and Grows in Holiness

---

⊀REVIEW⊁ Vocabulary
looked at one another in *consternation*   *relics*
too *sublime* for the average man   *excommunication*

??? Comprehension Questions/Narration Prompts
1. What caused the novices to believe that Hyacinth was a saint?
2. By what means did Bishop Stanislaus believe that we can become perfect?

💡 Forming Opinions/Drawing Conclusions
1. Describe in your own words Bishop Ivo's description of "The Way of the Cross" (pages 72-74). How can develop a more saintly attitude towards suffering and cheerful acceptance of your daily crosses?
2. The bishop accused King Boleslaus of breaking the fifth, sixth, seventh, and eighth commandments. Match the following actions of Boleslaus with the correct commandment he broke: stealing, lying, his cruelty in battle, and having more than one wife.

📖 For Further Study
Research the life of St. Stanislaus of Cracow, who was born in 1030, martyred in 1079, and canonized in 1253. Write a short biography of his life.

✝ Growing in Holiness
Unite yourself totally to the Holy Will of God by accepting daily the events, and sufferings He places before you. Accept His Will cheerfully and unquestioningly.

🗺 Geography
Add Sandomierz to your map. Draw a dashed orange line from Cracow to Sandomierz to show that Hyacinth traveled there.

✓ Checking the Catechism
Older students can read the *CCC*'s text paragraphs 541-42, 1809, and 2822-27 (91, 121, and 591) on following Jesus and the Will of God. Complete Activity #17 in *100 Activities*. Younger students may review the attributes (perfections) of God in their own catechisms.

📖 Searching Scripture
Hyacinth protested when the Duke prostrated himself before him. Read of a similar occurrence with Peter in Acts 10:25-26.

Chapter 8—In Which the Blessed Mother Agrees to Bless Hyacinth's Missionary Efforts, and He Promises to Promote Devotion to Her

✺REVIEW✺ Vocabulary

his friends were not *infallible*   *Te Deum*
repair to the monastery   *Provincial*

??? Comprehension Questions/Narration Prompts

1. List at least three miracles or cures attributed to Hyacinth in this chapter.
2. What would James have to give up in order to join the Dominicans?
3. What are the two promises of this chapter? Who made them?

Forming Opinions/Drawing Conclusions

1. Hyacinth states that when God is truly present in our hearts, it is easy to understand the true meaning of love. Why would this be true?
2. The Blessed Mother asks Hyacinth to teach souls to look upon her as a true mother. Explain what this means and how it can be accomplished.

For Further Study

Research the history of the Feast of the Assumption of Mary, celebrated since the seventh century. Read 1 Corinthians 15:50-58 on the glorification of the body. Pope Pius XII declared Mary's assumption—body and soul—into heaven to be a doctrine of the faith in 1950. The Feast of the Assumption (August 15) is a holy day of obligation in the United States. Write a short summary of your research.

Growing in Holiness

Recite the Litany of Saints; perhaps a lighted votive candle will assist in a prayerful recitation. Try to chant it as they may have done in Hyacinth's time.

Geography

Label the city of Constantinople on your map.

✓ Checking the Catechism

Older students can read text paragraphs 914-933 (192-193) of the *CCC* on the consecrated life. If desired, complete Activity #79 in *100 Activities*. Younger students may review vocations and the Sacrament of Holy Orders.

Searching Scripture

Hyacinth raised from the dead the only son of a widow just as Jesus did. Read Luke 7:11-17. Compare these two miracles.

Chapter 9–In Which Hyacinth Begins His Missionary Trips to Northern Europe

✖REVIEW✖ Vocabulary

he had no *scruples*

eking out a livelihood

missionaries

martyr

??? Comprehension Questions/Narration Prompts

1. Why were Florian, Godinus, and Benedict uneasy about following Hyacinth to Prussia?
2. How did Hyacinth cross the raging river Vistula? How did his three companions cross? What was the response of the people when they saw this miracle?

Forming Opinions/Drawing Conclusions

Pretend you are Florian. Describe your thoughts and feelings as you relay the events as they are happening when you cross the Vistula River on a cloak. Be dramatic as this was a dramatic event!

For Further Study

Research St. Adalbert, "Apostle of Prussia," who was martyred in 997. Present your research in an oral presentation or brief report.

Growing in Holiness

When asked by His apostles how they could increase their faith, Christ told them that if they had faith the size of a mustard seed, they could ask a tree to uproot itself into the sea and it would obey them (Luke 17:5-6). Begin to pray with more faith and ask God to increase your faith each day.

Geography

Add the following labels to your map in orange: Masovia in northern Poland (also known as Mazovia), and Gedan (also known as Sdansk or Danzig).

✓ Checking the Catechism

Older students should study the ten commandments in the *CCC* before text paragraph 2052 (434). If desired, complete Activity #59 in *100 Activities*. Younger students should review the commandments in their own catechisms. All students should be tested on their memorization of the commandments.

Searching Scripture

Read the account of Jesus walking on water from Matthew 14:22-33 as well as his calming of the storm in Matthew 8:23-27.

Chapter 10—In Which Hyacinth and His Companions Go to Russia

✴️REVIEW✴️ Vocabulary

justice to the *downtrodden*	*penitents*
as he *pondered* on this fact	*pagan*

⁇⁇ Comprehension Questions/Narration Prompts

1. What offering did Hyacinth ask Benedict to renew daily?
2. What made Russia such a fertile missionary country?
3. List the errors of the Russian Church.
4. What is the secret of the cross?

📖 For Further Study

Using *The Catechism of the Catholic Church* and the Bible, defend against the four points of heresy of the "eastern Catholics": the pope is not the vicar of Christ on earth, in Purgatory souls are not cleansed from the stain of sin, the bread and wine are not changed into the Body and Blood of Christ at the consecration, and the Holy Spirit does not proceed from both the Father and the Son. Choose one or two points, and create an outline with your defense.

✝️ Growing in Holiness

Hyacinth prayed that all may cherish the gift of the true Faith and understand the meaning of the Cross. Each evening before bed, place yourself on your knees before a crucifix. Recall any sins you may have committed that day and express your sorrow for each of them. To aid you in meditating upon the sacrifice of Jesus, imagine that the Body of Christ on the crucifix is still alive. Place yourself in His presence during His Passion. Always remember the depths of His love.

🗺️ Geography

Add the following cities to your map in orange: Kiev and Breslau.

✓ Checking the Catechism

Consider the difference between the cross of Good Friday and cross of Easter. Younger students can study the passion, death, and resurrection of our Lord. Older students may read text paragraphs 988-1019 (112, 118, and 202-206) in the *CCC*. Have younger students complete Activity #7 in *100 Activities*, while older students complete Activity #83.

📖 Searching Scripture

Florian stated that we must never cease from praying. Read Luke 18:1-8 to see what Jesus says about the necessity of praying always.

Chapter 11–In Which the Russian Priests Become Jealous of Hyacinth

---

✖REVIEW✖ Vocabulary

these *benighted* souls   *novitiate*
little more than crude *barbarians*   *eastern Catholics*

??? Comprehension Questions/Narration Prompts

1. What was the prophecy of Hyacinth regarding the monastery in Russia and the western priests?
2. How did Hyacinth cross the Dnieper River?
3. Who did Hyacinth attack when he went to help the pagans as they worshiped their idols?

Forming Opinions/Drawing Conclusions

1. "How mysterious the workings of grace!" (page 115) Why did Hyacinth feel that some new suffering would come because of the conversion of the Russian monarch, Vladimir? Are you part of this "real army" ready to assist those who wish to convert? What can you do to get ready? How can you provide this assistance?
2. What commandment of God were the pagans breaking by offering sacrifices to iron and stone statues?

For Further Study

"War was a dreadful matter, even when waged in a just cause" (page 119). Research in the *CCC* text paragraphs 2243 and 2309 (483-486), which summarize the four conditions necessary for a just war. Outline the elements of the "just war doctrine."

✝ Growing in Holiness

Memorize the prayer to St. Michael, which was composed by Pope Leo XII at the end of the nineteenth century as protection against the devil: "St. Michael the Archangel, defend us in the day of battle. Be our safeguard against the wickedness and snares of the devil. May God rebuke him we humbly pray, and do thou, Prince of the Heavenly Host, by the power of God, cast into hell Satan and all the other evil spirits that prowl through the world seeking the ruin of souls." This prayer used to be said after each Mass. Begin to say this prayer daily.

Searching Scripture

Read of Jesus' temptation by the devil in Matthew 4:1-11.

Chapter 12–In Which Hyacinth Leaves Russia and Continues His Journeys

---

✱REVIEW✱ Vocabulary

send this *meddling* westerner back   *Friars Preachers*

Carved piece of *alabaster*   *chapter*

??? Comprehension Questions/Narration Prompts

1. Within the city of Kiev, Hyacinth founded a religious community. Name other cities in which he founded religious communities.
2. Why did the death of Hyacinth's disciple Beranger bring Hyacinth great joy?
3. At what age did Hyacinth know the year of his death?

Forming Opinions/Drawing Conclusions

What virtues would be necessary in order to share with Hyacinth his attitude toward his own death as well as the death of those he loved? What can you do to cultivate these virtues? Why is it important to have an open, unafraid attitude toward death? Are you wisely using the time God has given you for His service?

For Further Study

Research the Tartar leaders, Genghis Khan and his grandson, Batu Khan. Include in your research Mangu Khan who is mentioned in the upcoming chapter. Prepare an oral presentation on these three men.

✝ Growing in Holiness

Hyacinth experienced JOY upon hearing of the deaths of his uncle Ivo and his beloved friend, Father Beranger, as it was the will of Jesus to take them, and they had gone to their reward. Hyacinth was able to put his own feelings of loss last. Remember that true joy comes only by keeping our priorities in proper order: <u>J</u>esus first, <u>O</u>thers second, and <u>Y</u>ourself last. This helps remind us how to experience true JOY.

Geography

Add these to your map in orange: Galicia, Denmark, Norway, Sweden, and Plock. Also add Dalmatia, where one of Hyacinth's followers lost his life.

Searching Scripture

In prayer, Hyacinth asked the Blessed Mother when he may see her face to face as her total beauty remains hidden to him. Read 1 Corinthians 13:12 to better understand St. Paul's thoughts on when we will see and know all things clearly. (Also see the poem "Mater Amabilis" on page 54 of this study guide.)

Chapter 13–In Which the Tartar Barbarians Invade Europe

✦REVIEW✦ Vocabulary
gorgeous *panorama* of golden domes
golden domes and *minarets*

Salve Regina
ciborium

❓❓❓ Comprehension Questions/Narration Prompts
1. What prompted the custom of singing the Salve Regina for dying religious?
2. Who was the only god of the Tartars?
3. What happened to the body of Stanislaus after he was martyred?
4. What did our Lady request of Hyacinth as he fled from the Tartars?

💡 Forming Opinions/Drawing Conclusions
1. Explain why martyrdom is called a "glorious crown." Why is it glorious and why is it referred to as a "crown"?
2. Why did Hyacinth take the consecrated Hosts in the ciborium with him as he fled from the Tartars?

📖 For Further Study
Research the life of St. Margaret of Antioch, virgin and martyr of the third century. Who were her persecutors? How did she die? In what countries was she venerated, especially during the holy wars of the eleventh century? Organize your research into a brief report.

✝ Growing in Holiness
In answer to the prayers of Hyacinth and the village people, God restored the crop destroyed by hail. Recall how Hyacinth prayed all night before the Blessed Sacrament—arms outstretched. Pray a decade or two of the rosary while kneeling with arms outstretched.

🗺 Geography
Add the following to your map in orange: Hungary, Vilna, and Finland.

✓ Checking the Catechism
Younger students should review those sections of their catechisms on the Mass, especially as related to the articles used in the Holy Sacrifice to better understand what Hyacinth took with him when the Tartars invaded. Older students should read text paragraphs 1345-55 and 1382-83 (271, 283-285, and 288) in the *CCC*. If desired, complete Activity #84 in *100 Activities*, "Articles Used in Worship." Younger students can complete Activity #13, "Things We See at Mass."

Chapter 14–In Which Poland Is Granted Some Peace from the Tartars

✖REVIEW✖ Vocabulary

fertile acres lay *pillaged* and burned   *monastery*
the *corpus* smashed   *canonized*

??? Comprehension Questions/Narration Prompts

1. What three miracles occurred as Hyacinth and his friars fled the Tartars?
2. What prompted Hyacinth to emphasize that children be taught about God?
3. What was Hyacinth's prediction regarding the return of the Tartars?
4. What did Hyacinth recommend people do rather than ask him for cures?

Forming Opinions/Drawing Conclusions

1. State why it is important for children to learn the catechism and discover the happiness found in trusting in the Holy Will of God. What else is important to know?
2. Hyacinth predicted several years of peace from the Tartars. But "what was truly permanent about *several years of peace*" (page 157)? Imagine what it might be like to live under those conditions. What aspects of your life would be affected?

For Further Study

Research the rise and fall of the Tartars; the word means "archer" or "nomad." Where did they originate? When did they found the Mongolian Empire? In the 1200's, what countries did they move through? Prepare a well-drafted outline on the Tartars.

✝ Growing in Holiness

Hyacinth asked, "Why not spend five minutes in honest prayer before the Blessed Sacrament" (page 162)? Go to church and pray before the Blessed Sacrament this week. Take a friend with you.

Geography

A different biographer, Sister Mary Jean Dorcy, places Hyacinth as a missionary in Moldavia, Livonia, Tibet, Chinese Turkestan, Tartary (Manchuria and Mongolia), and China. (See *Hunters of Souls, Dominican Saints and Blesseds*.) Other authors also add Scotland. Find these places on a larger map to fully comprehend the extent of Hyacinth's travels. Remember that he suffered the cold of the northern regions and the heat of the Gobi Desert—and all of his journeys were done on foot!

Chapter 15–In Which Hyacinth Continues Preaching and Founding Monasteries

---

✦REVIEW✦ Vocabulary

The *havoc* wrought   *vow*
officially *renounced* all missionary work   *episcopacy*

??? Comprehension Questions/Narration Prompts

1. Why did Hyacinth recommend consecration to our Lady?
2. What prayers did the Cistercian order offer for work of the Preaching Friars?
3. What was the pattern of Hyacinth's missionary life?
4. What did Hyacinth claim was necessary for salvation?

Forming Opinions/Drawing Conclusions

Explain why the gift of miraculous powers was best suited to converting pagans. Which gift would be most effective today for the conversion of sinners? Why? What would it be like to be a Christian living in a land where idols are openly worshipped? What gifts can you use to profess your faith and convert others?

✝ Growing in Holiness

Hyacinth felt that all children should be consecrated to our Lady. Recite the following prayer before the Blessed Sacrament; renew it each month on the first Saturday.

"O Exalted Mother of God, Queen of Heaven and Earth, Mother of our Lord Jesus Christ, I consecrate myself to thee this day and humbly ask thee to take me under thy constant care and protection as thy devoted child. O tender Mother of our Redeemer, fill me with thy love for your beloved Son and make me into a likeness of Him and thyself. Fashion my heart after thy heart. Make it tender, pure, gentle, and kind. Give me great reverence for life, and devotion to duty. O Spouse of the Holy Spirit, fill me with thy virtues that by the power of the Holy Spirit I may become a true spouse of Jesus Christ. O Star of the Sea, guiding light, ever guide me into a deeper union with Jesus that I may glorify Him in time and eternity for the greater glory of the Most Holy Trinity, now and forever. Amen." (Taken from *The Apostolate of Holy Motherhood*, published in 1991 by the Riehle Foundation)

Geography

Add the cities of Smolensk and Moscow to your map in orange.

📖 Searching Scripture

Read Mark 16:17 and Acts 2:4-11 regarding the gift of "tongues."

Chapter 16–In Which Hyacinth's Earthly Journey Ends

⬛REVIEW⬛Vocabulary
to *wrest* from the Divine Mercy   *Divine Mercy*
but to no *avail*   *Extreme Unction*

??? Comprehension Questions/Narration Prompts
1. How many years of missionary work did Hyacinth do?
2. How did the description of Hyacinth's vision of heaven aid his community?
3. What was St. Hyacinth's favorite devotion?

Forming Opinions/Drawing Conclusions
1. What significance did the Feast of the Assumption have for Hyacinth?
2. Explain John's exclamation from page 178, "If God grants what we ask, no one here will ever fall into grievous sin again!"

For Further Study
Review the completed map of Hyacinth's travels. Write a summary of his travels and the impact his missionary travels had on the spread of Christianity in northern Europe. (Be sure to include that he is attributed with 120,000 baptisms!)

✝ Growing in Holiness
Florian gives an example of service in this chapter—his service to the needs of Hyacinth. Determine to be a good servant and anticipate the needs of others. Do extra chores, and perform special kindnesses.

Geography
Locate the city in which St. Hyacinth, the Apostle of the North, died. Place an appropriate sticker (such as a gold star, a cross, or flower) on this city. Compare your completed map with a map of the modern world. List the cities on your map and write the corresponding countries to which they now belong.

Timeline Work
Add the events from 1238 through 1276 to complete your timeline.

✓ Checking the Catechism
Younger students can review the Sacrament of the sick (Extreme Unction or Anointing), while older students read text paragraphs 1511-23 (313-320) in the *CCC*. If desired, complete Activity #89 in *100 Activities* regarding anointing.

✎ Book Summary Test for *Saint Hyacinth*

Directions: Answer in complete sentences. If necessary, use the back of the page for additional writing space. 100 possible points, 20 points for each answer.

1. List at least three miracles attributed to Hyacinth during his lifetime.

    _____

    _____

    _____

2. To which religious order did Hyacinth and his companions belong? Give at least one other name for this order.

    _____

    _____

3. Name the "four apostles of the North." Explain how they came together and their relationship with one another.

    _____

    _____

    _____

4. Relate at least two instances in this book of the intercession of the Blessed Mother for Hyacinth.

    _____

    _____

    _____

5. Name several holy habits of St. Hyacinth's that you admire. Choosing at least one of these habits, relate your plan to incorporate this habit into your own daily life.

    _____

    _____

    _____

    _____

    _____

Saint Hyacinth of Poland, The Story of the Apostle of the North
Answer Key to Comprehension Questions

Chapter 1—In Which Hyacinth Becomes an Apostle for Poland
1. The story of how Father Dominic brought a dead man back to life is recorded in this chapter.
2. The bishop asked Father Dominic to provide some friars to become missionaries to Poland. Father Dominic responded by requesting the bishop to send the bishop's nephews and servants to Father Dominic for training in his order, so they might return to convert Poland themselves.

Chapter 2—In Which St. Dominic Trains the Four Apostles
1. Father Dominic required the members of his order to give up their possessions as well as their freedom to come and go and do. As a member of the Dominican order, a friar was required to give himself completely into God's hands (page 10).
2. The request for the love for souls is the one prayer that Hyacinth said God always hears—"If we ask Him, God will give us such a love for souls that we'll forget all about the suffering. . . . I'm sure this is one prayer He always hears" (page 12).
3. The two mottoes of the Dominican order are *Veritas*—Truth—and *Contemplare, et contemplata aliis tradere*—to contemplate and to give others the fruit of one's contemplation.

Chapter 3—In Which Hyacinth Tells the History of the Church in Poland
1. The distance from Rome, Italy, to Cracow (Krakow), Poland is about seven hundred fifty miles.
2. Herman prayed daily to our Lady (under the title of "Seat of Wisdom") that she would enlighten his mind and make him into a worthy friar.
3. Father Dominic predicted that this date would be the date of his own death.
4. Father Dominic did not fulfill his dream of becoming an Asian missionary as Pope Innocent III expressly forbade him to go. He did not accompany Hyacinth and his companions to Poland as he felt what strength he had left would be best spent on training others to become missionaries.

Forming Opinions/Drawing Conclusions
Three possibilities include St. Maximilian Kolbe, St. Faustina Kowalska, and Pope John Paul II.

Chapter 4—In Which the Four Apostles Leave St. Dominic
1. Father Dominic placed Hyacinth in charge of the four apostles.
2. The four friars stayed in monasteries as much as possible when traveling in order to offer the Holy Sacrifice of the Mass and to join others in prayer.

Chapter 5—In Which the Preaching and Sacrifices of the Four Apostles Begin to Be Rewarded
1. Hyacinth marveled that a Dominican monastery was built in a city in which Father Dominic had never visited, was filled to capacity in just a few months' time, and was founded by a priest before a year had passed since his ordination.
2. "Prayer is certainly the most wonderful medicine in the world" (page 47).
3. Prayer and work are the twin tools with which we build our ladder to heaven.

Chapter 6—In Which Hyacinth Reaches Cracow Alone
1. Hyacinth attributed sacrifice as the secret to Father Dominic's success as a preacher.
2. Hyacinth prophesizes that he would go to Poland, Ruthenia, Lithuania, and Prussia, and Ceslaus would preach in Bohemia, Silesia, and Germany.
3. Hyacinth feels that all men experience true peace in direct proportion to the amount in which they know, love, and do the Holy Will of God.

4. The Dominican nuns offered prayer and sacrifice to support the work of the Dominican priests.

For Further Study

This text can be found in Luke 22:42.

Chapter 7—In Which Hyacinth Establishes a Monastery in Cracow and Grows in Holiness

1. The novices believed that Hyacinth was a saint when they discover that Hyacinth had learned of Father Dominic's death via direct communication with God.
2. Bishop Stanislaus stated, "We can become perfect only by doing what Adam and Eve were too proud to do . . . [unite] ourselves to the Will of the Heavenly Father in all things—which means never questioning, even for an instant, the events He places in our daily lives" (pages 73-74).

Forming Opinions/Drawing Conclusions

The bishop accused the king of breaking the fifth commandment by his cruelty in battle, the sixth commandment by having more than one wife, the seventh commandment by stealing, and the eighth commandment by lying.

Chapter 8—In Which the Blessed Mother Agrees to Bless Hyacinth's Missionary Efforts, and He Promises to Promote Devotion to Her

1. The Miracles and cures of Hyacinth in this chapter include the following: the raising the boy Peter from the dead, the cure of a woman struck with paralysis, the cure of a woman of severe headaches, and the appearance of the Queen of Heaven to Hyacinth.
2. James would have to give up all his worldly possessions, profess obedience to his superior, and make a complete offering of himself to God.
3. The promise made by the Blessed Mother was that Hyacinth would bring the Faith to all of northern Europe. In turn, Hyacinth promised to bring souls to Mary and teach them to love her.

Chapter 9—In Which Hyacinth Begins His Missionary Trips to Northern Europe

1. Florian, Godinus, and Benedict were uneasy about accompanying Hyacinth to Prussia as it was isolated and full of pagan tribes known to be hostile to strangers—especially missionaries.
2. Hyacinth crossed the Vistula River by walking across the waves. The three missionaries crossed by riding upon the cloak of Hyacinth. The people responded by confessing their sins and promising to build a monastery for Hyacinth.

Chapter 10—In Which Hyacinth and His Companions Go to Russia

1. Hyacinth asked Benedict to renew the offering of himself to the Father every day—putting himself at the complete disposal of the Heavenly Father.
2. Russia was fertile mission territory as it had many churches and monasteries, but the Russian bishops and priests had been living in error for generations accepting only part of the truth of the Church. They had taught these errors to the people.
3. The errors being taught in Russia include the following: no recognition of the pope as Christ's vicar on earth, no belief in Purgatory, no belief in the True Presence of the Eucharist, and belief that the Holy Spirit proceeds only from the Father (a dispute begun with the addition of the *filioque*—"and from the Son"—to the Nicene Creed in 381).
4. The secret of the Cross is that when we accept our crosses readily, the suffering it brings becomes tinged with joy. When we complain, our souls become slaves to fear and pain (page 107).

Chapter 11—In Which the Russian Priests Become Jealous of Hyacinth

1. Hyacinth's prophecy regarding the Russian priests was that within two years several new priests would be ordained. Other priests would be converted and come to live in the new monastery.
2. Hyacinth crossed the Dnieper River by walking across the surface after flying down the hill.
3. Hyacinth was attacking a creature—half man, half beast—the devil himself.

Chapter 12—In Which Hyacinth Leaves Russia and Continues His Journeys

1. Besides Kiev, Hyacinth founded religious communities at Friesach, Olmutz, Cracow, Sandomierz, Troppau, and Gedan.
2. Hyacinth felt great joy at the death of his disciple as he felt that God would accept the sacrifice of Father Beranger's death by blessing the work of the Dominicans with true success.
3. At age fifty-one, Hyacinth knew that he had twenty-one more years of service to our Lord.

Chapter 13—In Which the Tartar Barbarians Invade Europe

1. The martyrdom of Ceslaus and forty-eight members of his community while singing the *Salve Regina* at Night Prayers (Compline) began the custom of singing this hymn at the death bed of every member of the Dominican order.
2. Hyacinth stated that the only god of the Tartars was the "god of war" (page 141).
3. The body of Stanislaus, who was killed by King Boleslaus, was cut into pieces and thrown into a field. Later, the clergy from the bishop's cathedral put together the pieces and hid them in a secret place. Before the burial, the pieces miraculously joined together.
4. The Blessed Virgin Mary spoke to Hyacinth and requested that he carry the alabaster statue of her as he was fleeing with the Blessed Sacrament in his other hand.

Chapter 14—In Which Poland Is Granted Some Peace from the Tartars

1. The three miracles that occurred while Hyacinth and his friars fled the invading Tartars are as follows: the lessening in weight of our Lady's statue, the miraculous escape from the Tartars, and the journey of Hyacinth with the friars down the river as they walked upon the water.
2. Hyacinth saw children as the hope of the future. He believed that they must be taught to know, love, and serve God to be happy in this world, to do God's work, and to prevent further wars.
3. Hyacinth predicted that the Tartars would return in 1259—two years after his death.
4. He recommended that they spend five minutes before the Blessed Sacrament in prayer.

Chapter 15—In Which Hyacinth Continues Preaching and Founding Monasteries

1. He believed that our Lady gave special graces to those in her care—especially little ones.
2. The Cistercians offered the following prayers to further the work of the Friars Preachers: Seven Psalms were to be recited daily by each of the priests, and seven Our Fathers were to be recited daily by each of the lay brothers.
3. In his missionary work, Hyacinth always founded as many monasteries as possible, placed a younger man in charge of each monastery, and then moved on to another place.
4. "All that is necessary for our salvation is to love God and to do His Will" (page 175).

Chapter 16—In Which Hyacinth's Earthly Journey Ends

1. Hyacinth was a missionary for thirty-seven years.
2. The members of Hyacinth's community began to look upon their work as a means to gain heaven and purchase eternal joy.
3. St. Hyacinth's favorite devotion was complete abandonment to the Divine Will.

Answer Key to Test

1. The following miracles are attributed to Hyacinth during his lifetime: the Blessed Virgin appeared and blessed Hyacinth upon his entrance into Cracow; Hyacinth brought Peter back to life after drowning; he cured a woman struck with paralysis; he cured a woman of severe headaches; the Queen of Heaven appeared to him and spoke to him; Hyacinth walked across the Vistula River and enabled his three companions to ride across on his cloak; he restored sight to Princess Anna; Hyacinth walked across the Dnieper River; he restored the crops from damage incurred by a hailstorm; Hyacinth—carrying the Blessed Sacrament in one

hand and a fifty-five pound statue in another—and his companions passed harmlessly through the hordes of Tartars as they fled Kiev; Hyacinth and his companions walked on the water downstream as they fled the Tartars; Hyacinth possessed the gift of prophecy as well as the gift of tongues; he restored sight to twin babies born without eyes; he raised Vislaus from the dead; he had a vision of heaven; and he predicted the year of his own death.

2. Hyacinth and his companions belonged to the Dominican order and were, in fact, accepted into the order by St. Dominic himself. Several other names include the Order of Preachers and Order of Friars Preachers.

3. The "four apostles of the North" include Hyacinth and his brother Ceslaus as well as Herman and Henry, two of their uncle's lay attendants. Ceslaus became prior in Prague in 1220 and traveled to Bohemia, Silesia (Breslau), Germany and other places; he is attributed with several miracles before dying on July 17, 1242. Herman (the Teuton of Germany) became the prior at the monastery in Friesach, Austria, in 1220 and died on April 17, 1245. Henry of Moravia began a monastery in Olmutz in 1220 and later another in Breslau; he died around 1245. Hyacinth himself traveled throughout northern Europe, as far east as northern China, south to Greece, west as far as Scotland, and north into Sweden, and Norway—all on foot! He is credited with the baptism of 120,000 pagans and numerous miracles. He died on August 15, 1257. (NOTE: Some of the above information comes from outside sources. Accept much more basic information for full credit.)

4. Hyacinth had a great devotion (perhaps influenced by St. Dominic himself) to the mother of God. The Blessed Mother intervened for Hyacinth numerous times in his life. She interceded for him when he asked that Peter's life be restored to him. The Blessed Virgin appeared to Hyacinth and promised him that his wish to evangelize all of northern Europe would be granted. She helped him and his companions cross the raging Vistula River. She also spoke to him in Kiev, asking him to take her statue with him while she asked Jesus to ease the heavy load of the statue.

5. Answers will vary.

Study Guide for

Saint Louis de Montfort, The Story of Our Lady's Slave

St. Louis de Montfort

Louis was born the second of eighteen
A son born in France to John and to Jean.
His destiny clear,
Pursued without fear,
The priesthood to serve sweet Mary our Queen.

In Poiters he arrived, chaplain to the poor,
To Jesus through Mary gave graces galore.
A slave to Mary,
Made many wary,
The rosary, the saints—these he could not ignore.

The Jansenists hated him, wanted him out.
He spoke to the people, spoke with great clout.
Simple was his way,
God's will did convey,
Heretics ousted him, his motives in doubt.

Pope Clement insisted—to France he returned.
Although to the New World, St. Louis had yearned.
Preached, suffered, and prayed,
And always obeyed.
To west central France as a missioner sojourned.

His doctrines and teachings were always well grounded.
Yet by the Jansenists he still was hounded.
The Calvinists too,
As critics he drew.
Orders for priests and sisters he founded.

St. Louis de Montfort obeyed without fuss.
His humble manner was always a plus.
Despite enemies made,
Foundations he laid.
Devotion to Mary established for us.

Think what you can learn from this saint and his tale.
How you can apply it to help you prevail.
Then mold what you do
And boldly pursue
His pattern of holiness. Follow his trail.

Timeline of Events

Year	Event
1670	First minute hands on watches
1673	Birth of Louis Grignion de la Rachelleraie in Montfort, France on January 31st; Marquette and Joliet reach headwaters of Mississippi
1675	Paris becomes the center of European culture with a half million inhabitants
1682	William Penn founds Quaker colony in Pennsylvania
1685	Louis begins school at St. Thomas Becket with the Jesuit Fathers at Rennes
1688	Death of John Bunyan, author of *The Pilgrim's Progress*
1693	Louis goes to Paris to study; enters St. Sulpice Seminary in July of 1695
1696	St. Alphonsus de Liguori born; dies in 1787; declared Doctor of Church in 1871
1700	Louis-Marie (a name taken at Confirmation) ordained as a priest on June 5th
1701	Father de Montfort assigned as chaplain at public hospital at Poiters in November
1703	February 2nd, habit given to Mary-Louise Trichet, first sister of the Congregation of the Daughters of Wisdom; Father de Montfort leaves Poiters in April for Paris
1704	Father de Montfort writes *Love of Eternal Wisdom;* returns to Poiters in March
1706	In March, Father de Montfort forbidden by the bishop of Poiters to preach in the diocese; travels to Rome to consult Pope Clement XI who entitles him as "Apostolic Missionary"; begins to preach in Brittany
1708	In May, Father de Montfort goes to work in the diocese of Nantes
1709	In April begins mission at Pontchâteau; begins construction of the Calvary shrine there, which is completed in August of 1710 and shortly thereafter destroyed
1710	Father de Montfort joins the Dominican order as a tertiary on November 10th
1711	Louis de Montfort leaves Nantes to preach in the dioceses of La Rochelle and Luçon, in the Vendée region of France; consumes poisoned soup in August; music of Johann Sebastian Bach and George Frederick Handel popular
1712	Father de Montfort writes his book, *True Devotion to the Blessed Virgin Mary*
1714	Father de Montfort writes *Letter to Friends of the Cross*; D.G. Fahrenheit constructs the mercury thermometer with temperature scale
1715	First priest, Father Adrian Vatel, joins Father de Montfort's Company of Mary
1716	Father Louis de Montfort dies on April 28th in St.-Laurent-sur-Sèvre, France
1732	Benjamin Franklin's "Poor Richard's Almanack" issued (until 1757)
1753	Liberty Bell is hung Philadelphia and cracks with the first stroke of the clapper
1776	American Revolutionary War fought (until 1883)
1786	Jean-Marie Vianney, later the Curé of Ars, born on May 8th in Dardilly, France
1789	French Revolution begins (to 1799); John Carroll named bishop of Baltimore
1799	Napoleon Bonaparte comes to power in France; Pauline Jaricot born in Lyons, France; ban lifted on religious practices in France in 1802
1803	President Jefferson secures the Louisiana Purchase for the United States
1842	On April 22nd, the finding of the manuscript, and subsequent publication, of True Devotion to the Blessed Virgin Mary as written by Louis de Montfort
1861	Beginning of the United States Civil War (until 1865)
1888	Beatification of Father Louis de Montfort, January 22nd, by Pope Leo XIII; canonization of St. Louis-Marie Grignion de Montfort on July 20, 1947, by Pope Pius XII

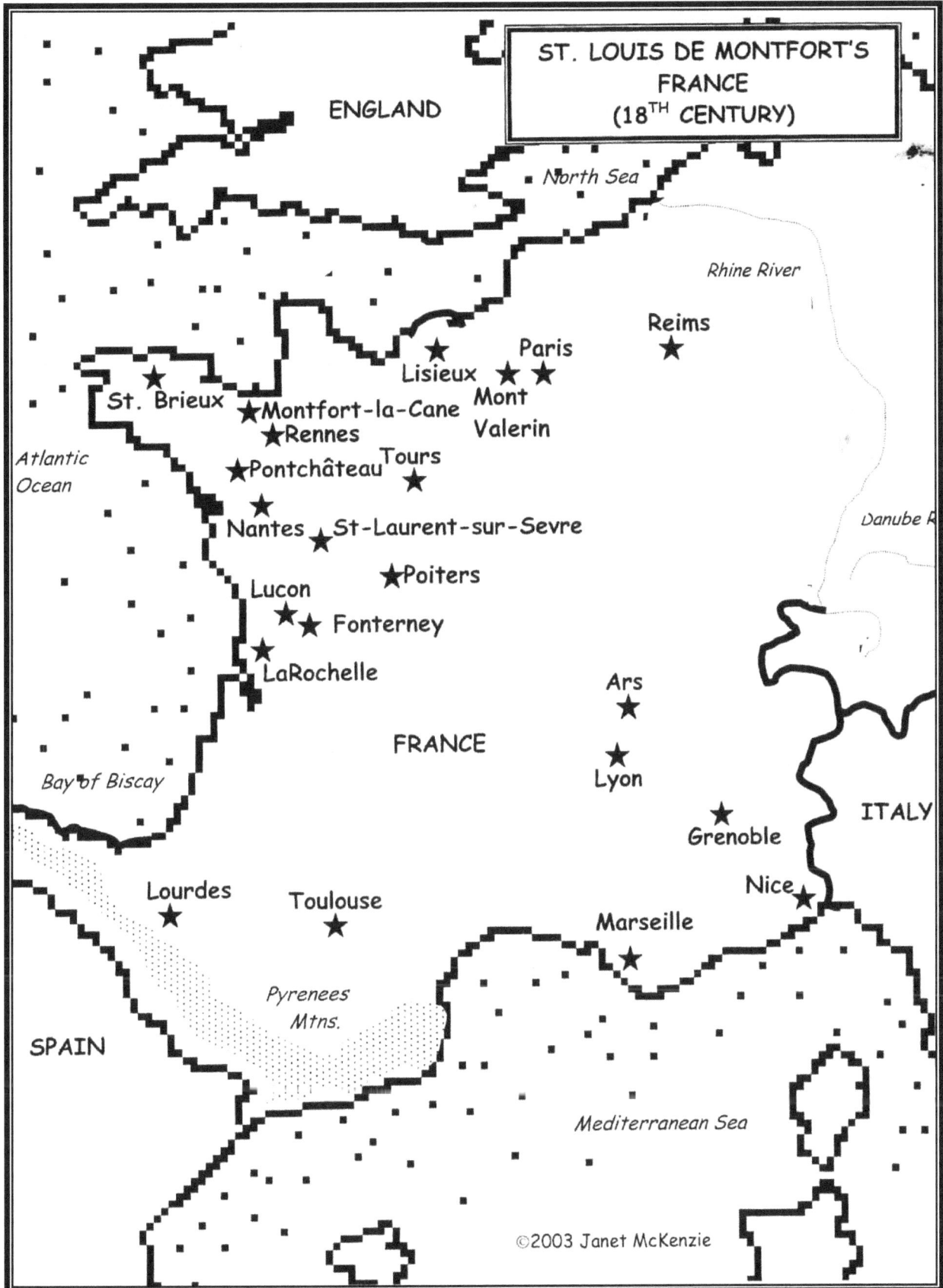

ST. LOUIS DE MONTFORT'S
FRANCE
(18TH CENTURY)

ENGLAND

North Sea

Rhine River

Reims

Paris

Lisieux

★ St. Brieux

★ Montfort-la-Cane
★ Rennes

Mont
Valerin

Atlantic
Ocean

★ Pontchâteau

Tours

★ Nantes

★ St-Laurent-sur-Sevre

★ Poiters

Lucon
★★ Fonterney

Danube R

Ars

★ LaRochelle

FRANCE

★ Lyon

Bay of Biscay

ITALY

Grenoble

Nice ★

Lourdes

Toulouse

Marseille

Pyrenees
Mtns.

SPAIN

Mediterranean Sea

©2003 Janet McKenzie

Chapters 1 through 4—In Which Father Grignion Is Assigned as Chaplain at the Poorhouse and Disappears

---

⭐REVIEW⭐ Vocabulary

... the word "slaves" is *repulsive*   *Sulpicians*

The matron *was anxious to show Father*   *Daughters of Charity*

??? Comprehension Questions/Narration Prompts

1. What did the monsignor find different about Father Grignion?
2. What did Father Grignion do to make enemies of the staff at the poorhouse?
3. What additional duties did Father Grignion take on within the city?

💡 Forming Opinions/Drawing Conclusions

1. The bishop of Poitiers stated that Father Grignion is "either a fool or a saint" (page 1). What is it about our Christian faith that makes those two very different terms seem at times to be so closely linked?
2. In what ways can Father Grignion be compared to Blessed Mother Teresa of Calcutta? (For further information on the sainthood cause of Blessed Mother Teresa, see www.motherteresa.org/Novena/MadreTeresa_feast_2008.html.)

✝ Growing in Holiness

Think of how often we, perhaps unwittingly, judge others by appearances—just as Father Grignion was judged when he first came to the poorhouse (page 6). Try to set aside exterior appearances, realizing that Christ Himself lives in others.

Geography

Trace the map on page 79 of this study guide. Label and color the four seas and oceans blue as well as the two rivers. Label the Pyrenees Mountains and color them brown. (This map will be completed in Chapters 16-19 and 24-27.)

✓ Checking the Catechism

Older students may learn more about the slavery of sin in the *Catechism of the Catholic Church* (*CCC*) by reading text paragraphs 421, 549, 1733, 1741, and 2097 (108 and 363).

📖 Searching Scripture

"Servant" and "slave" are used interchangeably in scripture as both derive from the Hebrew word "*'ebed*." Read these references to the servants or slaves of God: Mark 10:44, John 15:15, Galatians 1:10, and Revelation (Apocalypse) 1:1. (One title for the pope is the "slave [or servant] of the slaves of God.") Read references to being slaves to sin in John 8:31-36 and Romans 6:17-22. Read 1 Samuel (1 Kings) 16:7 on appearances.

Chapters 5 through 8–In Which Father de Montfort Returns and Begins to Preach True Devotion to the Blessed Virgin Mary

⭐REVIEW⭐ Vocabulary

on the *wane*   *act of consecration*
so wonderful, so *stupendous*   *spiritual director*

⁇⁇ Comprehension Questions/Narration Prompts

1. What was the Wisdom Group that Father Grignion established?
2. Why did Father Grignion assume the name "Father de Montfort"?
3. How long did Father de Montfort have Mary Louise prepare before he allowed her to formally make the Act of Consecration? Of what three people did he ask her to obtain more knowledge?

💡 Forming Opinions/Drawing Conclusions

1. Why does *The Baltimore Catechism* stress the importance to "know, love and serve"? Why are all three important in that particular order?
2. Why do you think Mary Louise was "scandalized at the mere idea of talking to our Lady as though she were a real person" (page 28)? How can you use this insight to enrich your own prayer life?

✝ Growing in Holiness

Design an original litany to St. Louis de Montfort by creating a summary title for him for each chapter. For example for chapters 1-4, use the following: "Fool of Christ," "Slave of Jesus in Mary," "Helper of the Poor," and "Generous Sufferer." Continue this litany construction throughout the remaining chapters. (Refer to a Catholic prayer book for examples of opening and closing prayers for your saint litany.)

📅 Timeline Work

Taping sheets of plain paper end-to-end, make a timeline representing the years from 1670 through 1888. Let three inches equal 25 years. Mark on your timeline the dates and events from 1670 through 1708, using information from page 78 of this study guide.

✓ Checking the Catechism

Older students may read the Church's teaching on merit in the following text paragraphs of the *CCC*: 956, 1476, 2006-11, and 2025-27 (312 and 426-427). If desired, complete Activity #72 in *100 Activities Based on the Catechism of the Catholic Church* (*100 Activities*). Younger students may study in their own catechisms on this same topic; additionally, review the catechism's references to the Blessed Virgin May.

Chapters 9 through 12–In Which Father de Montfort Founds the Daughters of Wisdom

---

✦REVIEW✦ Vocabulary

since she has no *dowry*   *Daughters of Wisdom*
taken aback by the Bishop's brusqueness   *Jansenists*

??? Comprehension Questions/Narration Prompts

1. How did Mary Louise's parents react when she asked permission to join Father de Montfort at the poorhouse? What reason did she give them for wanting to join?
2. Describe Mary Louise's "Baptism" for her new dress.

Forming Opinions/Drawing Conclusions

1. "How good not to belong to herself any more!" (page 41) What does this mean?
2. Compare and contrast the lifestyle of Mary Louise at the poorhouse (as described on pages 48-49) with an ordinary lifestyle at home and a typical schedule for a religious community. What do you think attracted her to this life?
3. Summarize in your own words the beliefs and heresies of the Jansenists. (See Father John Laux's description on pages 502-505 of his book, *Church History*.)

For Further Study

Research the religious order of the Daughters of Wisdom, their history, and their current standing. How did the French Revolution affect this order? Information can be obtained online at www.montfort.org.

✝ Growing in Holiness

On page 60, Father de Montfort discussed with Mary Louise the importance not only of a solid education in the doctrines of the church (catechism) but also the necessity of having the faith mean more than mere attendance at Mass on Sunday. He encouraged her us to pray for all priests, praying especially to the Blessed Virgin that she may enlighten their minds. Be sure to put into action each of these ideas.

✓ Checking the Catechism

Older students should read the *CCC* teachings on persecution in the following text paragraphs: 675, 769, and 1816.

▭ Searching Scripture

Mary Louise endured the misunderstanding of her mother and the persecution of the townspeople. Read what Holy Scripture has to say about persecution in Matthew 5:11-12 and Matthew 10:16-33. What does this mean for you as a Christian?

Chapters 13 through 15–In Which Father de Montfort Leaves, Returns, and Again Leaves Poiters

✖REVIEW✖ Vocabulary

Father de Montfort smiled *ruefully*   cassock
most *repugnant* to human nature   *free will*

??? Comprehension Questions/Narration Prompts

1. What was Father de Montfort's secret ambition since the seminary?
2. What did Father de Montfort do in his search for God's Will?
3. How did Father de Montfort gain the respect of the hermits of Mont Valérien?

Forming Opinions/Drawing Conclusions

1. ". . . the Calvary on Mont Valérien—that huge outdoor group of figures and crosses representing the death of Christ between two thieves. . . . There'd be far fewer sinners in France if every town could have a Calvary like that" (page 71). Why do you think Father de Montfort would make this statement? Do you think this statement could be made today about our country as well?
2. One Hail Mary said well each day is enough when praying for someone (page 76). What does this say, first of all, about the power of the Blessed Virgin's intercession, and, secondly, about God's willingness to grant our petitions?

For Further Study

Research the seventh-century saint, St. Sulpitius the Pious, from whom the Society of St. Sulpice (as well as the seminary in Paris) derives its name. Do not get confused with the sixth-century saint with a similar name, St. Sulpitius the Severe. (Note that sometimes these saints' names are spelled "Supicius.")

✝ Growing in Holiness

The professors at the Seminary of St. Sulpice argued that the idea of consecration to the Blessed Virgin was too different and unnecessary. They contended that "there must be thousands of canonized saints who never heard of it" (page 63). The Catholic Church offers many different ways to holiness. Remember when we study and imitate the saints that it is not necessary to utilize all of these means of grace, but to find our own path to holiness that is suited best for each of us. Incorporate those aspects of the saints' habits that seem most beneficial to your own spirituality.

✓ Checking the Catechism

"Even God Himself can't force the free will of one of His creatures" (page 76). Read the following text paragraphs 1730-40 (56, 358 and 363-366) of the *CCC* which teach about man's free will.

Chapters 16 through 19–In Which Father de Montfort Begins His Street Preaching in Earnest and Incurs the Wrath of the Jansenists

✴REVIEW✴ Vocabulary

by *dint* of their own prayers   *Francis of Assisi*
made a *vulgar*, straw-filled figure   *Vicar General*

⁇⁇ Comprehension Questions/Narration Prompts

1. What did Father de Montfort believe to be the easiest way to know, love, and serve God?
2. How did Father de Montfort win God's blessing on his work when giving missions and wresting souls from the hands of the devil?

💡 Forming Opinions/Drawing Conclusions

1. In these chapters, Father de Montfort began his "street preaching" in earnest. It is not necessary to be a priest to do this. What are some practical ways that we too can preach the Good News to people that we meet?
2. Brother Mathurin stated, "I like the word 'slave'" (page 90). What does it mean for you to be a "slave of Jesus"?
3. Why do you suppose the Jansenists were so opposed to Father de Montfort and his method of obtaining heaven?
4. List the virtues that Father de Montfort displayed when the Vicar General chastised him in front of the congregation of the Church of Calvary.

📦 For Further Study

Research the Capuchin order as mentioned on page 88. Of what order is it a branch? When was it founded, by whom, and why? Write a brief report or outline.

✝ Growing in Holiness

For one week pray the rosary as Father de Montfort did with the people of Montbernage—the Joyful Mysteries in the morning, the Sorrowful Mysteries at noon, and the Glorious Mysteries in the evening. (For two or three days, you could also substitute the Luminous Mysteries for one of the other three.) You need not prepare a chapel as these people did (page 84), but establish a special place within your home as a shrine to our Lady complete with a small statue or picture.

🗺 Geography

Continue the map started in Chapters 1-4 by labeling all cities red and the four countries green. On the map provided, cities are indicated with a star, and countries are in bold capitals.

Chapters 20 through 23–In Which Pope Clement XI Blesses Father de Montfort's Vocation of Preaching, Prayer, and Suffering

⭐REVIEW⭐Vocabulary

in *league* with the Devil
cut him to the *quick*

Basilica of the Holy House of Nazareth
plenary indulgence

??? Comprehension Questions/Narration Prompts

1. Father de Montfort traveled to Rome to discuss what topic with the Pope Clement XI? What was the Pope's response to Father's request?
2. What did the bishop of Poitiers tell Father de Montfort upon his return from Rome?

Forming Opinions/Drawing Conclusions

1. Compare and contrast the lives of St. Dominic and St. Louis de Montfort.
2. We are those unborn people of whom Father de Montfort speaks on pages 116-17. Write a letter to Father de Montfort and Brother Mathurin thanking them for the price they paid for you. Outline in this letter the specific sacrifices of theirs that you appreciate and the graces you feel you have obtained because of them.

For Further Study

Research the term "mission" (or "popular mission") used in the context of Father de Montfort's work. Use a Catholic dictionary or encyclopedia or talk to your parish priest. When is the last time a mission was offered at your parish?

✝ Growing in Holiness

Re-read Father de Montfort's exhortation on True Devotion to Mary and suffering (bottom of page 101 and continuing to page 102). How can you live out this idea in your daily life? What can you do to help yourself routinely remember to practice devotion to Mary as well as to embrace suffering?

✓ Checking the Catechism

Father de Montfort had contrite sinners renew their baptismal vows. Older students may read pertinent text paragraphs in the *CCC*: 1254, 2101-02, and 2340 (259 and 443). A plenary indulgence (with usual conditions) is granted for renewing your baptismal vows on the anniversary date of your baptism. What is the anniversary date of your baptism?

📖 Searching Scripture

"He must be in league with the devil to work so many wonders!" (page 100) These words were spoken about Jesus too. Read Luke 11:14-23.

Chapters 24 through 27–In Which Father de Montfort's Preaching and Example Convert Many People, But He Still Continues to Make Enemies

✶REVIEW✶ Vocabulary

was an *eminent* member   *Order of Friars Preachers*
was a *legend* in the neighborhood   *pulpit*

??? Comprehension Questions/Narration Prompts

1. What specific four promises did the Blessed Virgin make to Blessed Alan concerning the rewards in store for those who say the rosary devoutly?
2. Explain the habit of the Dominican brothers and priests.
3. What was the legend of the prophecy of St. Vincent Ferrer regarding the chapel of Our Lady of Pity?
4. Why was Father de Montfort asked to leave Brittany?

Forming Opinions/Drawing Conclusions

1. Explain the title of Chapter 24, "Discovered!" To what does this refer?
2. Why do you think Father de Montfort was reluctant to tell people who he was?

For Further Study

Research the life of Blessed Alan de la Roche (Alanus de Rupe). Where and when was he born, what was his religious order, and for what is he known?

✝ Growing in Holiness

Compare the measure of your obedience and humility to that displayed by Father de Montfort in the incident with Father Ledeuger on page 138. Ask Jesus to teach you the art of not excusing yourself. Do not forget to practice this art!

Geography

Research the dioceses and provinces of France. Use a Catholic or secular encyclopedia, use www.en.wikipedia.org/wiki/List_of_the_Roman_Catholic_dioceses_of_France, or conduct your own online search. Add regional titles to the map started in Chapters 1-4 by writing the names of the major provinces in orange and the dioceses connected with Father de Montfort (west central France) in purple.

📖 Searching Scripture

Locate these references in the Bible: two ordinary people seeking shelter from village people and being refused (page 121), a man contradicted and laughed at (page 133), and the passage quoted on page 135 regarding invitations to a dinner.

Chapters 28 through 31–In Which Father de Montfort and His Friends Continue to Be Misunderstood and Their Virtue Tested

---

REVIEW Vocabulary

make . . . grievance sound more *plausible*   *Calvary*

gave themselves to the *arduous* task   *baptismal vows*

??? Comprehension Questions/Narration Prompts

1. Who was the "new companion" of Chapter 28?
2. Why did Father de Montfort and his companions go to Nantes?
3. Father de Montfort received a very clear and immediate answer to his prayer for guidance on the building site for the Calvary shrine. What was this sign?
4. The Nantes' bishop had the Calvary destroyed and revoked his permission for Father de Montfort to preach and hear confessions. What did Father decide to do?

Forming Opinions/Drawing Conclusions

1. What is the relationship between prayer and action? Which is more important?
2. Describe the Calvary at Pontchâteau. Why was it built?

Growing in Holiness

Father de Montfort begged the Blessed Mother to "grant your choicest gifts to all who journey here in your honor" (page 142). Pilgrimage to a shrine of the Blessed Mother near your home. While there, pray the rosary, attend Mass, and make the Stations of the Cross. Ask Mary to bestow her choicest gifts upon your family.

Timeline Work

Add the dates and events from 1709 through 1712 to your timeline.

✓ Checking the Catechism

These chapters center around the cross—the cross as the primary symbol on the hillside at Pontchâteau and the crosses that Father de Montfort patiently bears. Read about the cross in the *CCC* in text paragraphs 598, 1366, 1435, 1816, 2015, 2029, 2157, and 2427 (110, 122, 280, and 428). If desired, complete Activity #4, in *100 Activities*. Younger students may review their catechisms' references to the stations of the cross and acts of penance.

Searching Scripture

Read the narrative of the Way of the Cross in Matthew 27:27-66. Read too what Holy Scripture teaches about obedience to ecclesiastical superiors: Matthew 23:1-3, Luke 10:16, Hebrews 13:17, and 1 Peter 5:5.

Chapters 32 through 35–In Which Father de Montfort Battles the Calvinists and Works to Build His Dream of the Company of Mary

✖REVIEW✖ Vocabulary

went so far as to *waylay* Father   *Minims*
had not the slightest *qualm*   *Company of Mary*

⁇⁇ Comprehension Questions/Narration Prompts

1. Although the influence of Jansenism was less widespread in the Dioceses of Lucon and LaRochelle, what other heresy did Father de Montfort have to battle?
2. Name the four brothers in the company of Father de Montfort around 1712.
3. Why did Father de Montfort go to Paris in August of 1713? Where did he plan to stop on his return trip?

💡 Forming Opinions/Drawing Conclusions

1. In your own words, explain what a third order religious—a tertiary—is. Name some religious orders that have a third order.
2. "Father de Montfort was like a thundering prophet from the pages of the Old Testament" (page 163). What image does this call to mind? Draw this image of Father de Montfort. Name several "thundering prophets" from the Old Testament.
3. Explain why it seems harder for people well-grounded in their faith to respond to the simplicity of the doctrines of True Devotion than new converts.

📖 For Further Study

St. Bernard had a great devotion to our Lady. Research his life, the times in which he lived, and his achievements for the Church.

✝ Growing in Holiness

The incident with the pirates in Chapter 34 is a perfect example of faith under pressure. Unless we rely on our faith in small matters, we will not have the faith and courage to use it when it is "crunch time." Practice talking to God and relying on the intercession of our Lady for little things. It will then come more easily in times of great importance.

✓ Checking the Catechism

One of Bishop de Champflour's canons stated that many people are against the True Devotion "because it is so simple" (page 165). Simplicity (having no parts and therefore indivisible) is one of the perfections of God. Read about this topic in the *CCC* in text paragraphs 41-42, 202, and 213. Or review the perfections of God in your own catechism.

Chapters 36 through 39–In Which Sister Mary Louise Moves to La Rochelle, The Company of Mary Grows, and Father Louis de Montfort Dies

---

✖REVIEW✖ Vocabulary
had a *veritable* passion for dancing   *zeal*
little time for idle *musing*   *indulgenced*

??? Comprehension Questions/Narration Prompts
1. What was the "surprise for Sister Mary Louise" of Chapter 36?
2. What was "The Bargain" of Chapter 38?
3. What attainments did Father de Montfort feel he had to show God upon his death?
4. What reportedly were the last words of Father Louis de Montfort?

Forming Opinions/Drawing Conclusions
1. "We ought to do everything possible to make the True Devotion known to young people" (page 185). What can you do to help spread this devotion to others?
2. "I'm just helping to pay the price. . . . Dearest Mother, please don't let me spoil things by complaining!" (page 186) What does this mean? How can you apply this idea?

For Further Study
Obtain some of the following books by and about St. Louis de Montfort and continue your study of him and his spirituality: *True Devotion to the Blessed Virgin* and its companion book, *Preparation for Total Consecration According to Saint Louis de Montfort*; *The Queen's Way* , a simplified version of *True Devotion*; *The Secret of the Rosary*, excellent meditation material; *The Secret of Mary*, an abridgement of *True Devotion*; *The Secret of Mary Explained to Children*, for grades two through eight; *Leading the Little Ones to Mary*, for grades one through three; *Letter to the Friends of the Cross*, a summary of the doctrine of the Cross; *Love of Eternal Wisdom*, which stresses the love God has for human beings; and *God Alone*, the collected works of de Montfort (includes some of the 164 de Montfort hymns that have been preserved).

✚ Growing in Holiness
"What *does* God want of me?" (page 190) Ask this question of yourself frequently. Prayerfully inquire of God Himself whether or not you are fulfilling His will.

📖 Searching Scripture
"But how often she had found only rocky soil for the priceless seed which she had to sow!" (page 184) Read this parable and Jesus' explanation of the parable in Holy Scripture in Matthew 13:1-9 and 18-23.

Epilogue–In Which the Company of Mary and the Daughters of Wisdom Carry on the Work of Father Louis de Montfort

✖REVIEW✖ Vocabulary

would *defray* the cost of repairs   *processions*
darkness and silence of a *coffer*   *motherhouse*

??? Comprehension Questions/Narration Prompts

1. What was the "little trick" that the pastor played on Father Mulot and Father Vatel?
2. By 1940, into what countries did St. Louis de Montfort's orders expand?

💡 Forming Opinions/Drawing Conclusions

What is the irony of Father Mulor and Father Vatel encouraging people to "have great faith in the Blessed Virgin and to ask her help in every difficulty" (page 204)?

📖 For Further Study

Research the current status of the Company of Mary using a Catholic encyclopedia or online encyclopedia at www.newadvent.org/cathen, or at www. montfort.org.

✝ Growing in Holiness

Consider sincerely making the Act of Consecration to the Blessed Virgin. Use the resources listed in the previous lesson—or see page 92 of this study guide for information on obtaining a free Marian consecreation packet. Complete and pray the litany to St. Louis de Montfort as begun on page 82 of this guide.

Geography

Check to ensure that the following dioceses are located on your map: Nantes, Lucon, LaRochelle, Poiters, Saint-Brieuc, Rennes, and Vannes.

Timeline Work

Add the dates and events from 1714 through 1888 to complete your timeline.

✓ Checking the Catechism

The pastor of Loges reflects on the "making of their Easter duty" (page 203). Every Catholic is required to receive the Holy Eucharist worthily during the Easter season. (In the United States this is from the first Sunday of Lent through Trinity Sunday—the first Sunday after Pentecost.) Read the *CCC* text paragraph 2042 (432). Research in your catechism which precepts of the Church cover the "Easter Duty."

St. Louis De Montfort's "Prayer To Jesus"

O most loving Jesus, let me pour forth my gratitude before You, for the grace You have bestowed upon me in giving me to Your holy Mother through the devotion of Holy Bondage, that she may be my advocate in the presence of Your majesty and my support in my extreme misery. Alas, O Lord! I am so wretched that without this dear Mother I should be certainly lost. Yes, Mary is necessary for me at Your side and everywhere; that she may appease Your just wrath, because I have so often offended You; that she may save me from the eternal punishment of Your justice, which I deserve; that she may help me to save my soul and the souls of others; in short, Mary is necessary for me that I may always do Your holy will and seek Your greater glory in all things. Ah, would that I could proclaim throughout the whole world the mercy that You have shown to me! Would that everyone might know I should be already damned, were it not for Mary! Would that I might offer worthy thanksgiving for so great a blessing! Mary is in me. Oh, what a treasure! Oh, what a consolation! And shall I not be entirely hers? Oh, what ingratitude! My dear Savior, send me death rather than such a calamity, for I would rather die than live without belonging entirely to Mary. With St. John the Evangelist at the foot of the cross, I have taken her a thousand times for my own and as many times have given myself to her; but if I have not yet done it as You, dear Jesus, would wish, I now renew this offering as You would desire me to renew it. And if You see in my soul or my body anything that does not belong to this august princess, I pray You to take it and cast it far from me, for whatever in me does not belong to Mary is unworthy of Thee.

O Holy Spirit, grant me all these graces. Plant in my soul the Tree of true Life, which is Mary; cultivate it and tend it so that it may grow and blossom and being forth the fruit of life in abundance. O Holy Spirit, give me great devotion to Mary, Your faithful spouse; give me great confidence in her maternal heart and an abiding refuge in her mercy, so that by her You may truly form in me Jesus Christ, great and mighty, into the fullness of His perfect age. Amen.

How To Obtain A Free Marian Consecration Packet

To receive a free packet of information on how to make your total consecration to Immaculate Mary, email your mailing address to Dick Sohm at RWSKOI@aol.com. This packet includes a thirty-day St. Louis de Montfort preparation prayer book, an audio tape, and the Holy Father's own consecration prayer. It can also be ordered from The Children of the Father Foundation, 222 S. Manoa Road, #250, Haverton, PA 19083. Recommended cycles of prayer to begin this consecration (with the consecration itself falling on one of Mary's feasts days) include December 31 through February 2nd, February 20 through March 25th, March 26th through April 28th, April 28th through May 31st, July 13th through August 15th, and November 5th through December 8th.

✎ Book Summary Test for *Saint Louis de Montfort*

Directions: Answer in complete sentences. If necessary, use the back of the page for additional writing space. 100 possible points, 20 points for each answer.

1. What was it about St. Louis de Montfort's preaching style that made so many enemies in eighteenth-century France?

   _____

   _____

2. What two main groups or heresies did St. Louis de Montfort battle in the various dioceses in which he preached?

   _____

   _____

   _____

3. Describe St. Louis de Montfort's doctrine of True Devotion to the Blessed Virgin.

   _____

   _____

4. List the accomplishments of St. Louis de Montfort—his writings, the orders he founded, his legacy of faith.

   _____

   _____

   _____

5. Name three practical actions that you can take or three habits that you can cultivate that would incorporate the teachings of St. Louis de Montfort in your own spiritual life.

   _____

   _____

   _____

Saint Louis de Montfort, The Story of Our Lady's Slave
Answer Key to Comprehension Questions

Chapters 1 through 4—In Which Father Grignion Is Assigned as Chaplain at the Poorhouse and Disappears

1. The monsignor (along with Father Grignion's former superiors) was uncomfortable with Father Grignion as he did not care about his outward appearance and dress. Elegance and prestige did not impress Father Grignion. Furthermore, he was not embarrassed or ashamed to be seen praying in public places. His attitude was different than other priests.
2. Father Grignion made enemies of the poorhouse staff as they believed he was pampering the poor by providing meat more often, blankets with which to sleep, and a clean place to live. The staff was not accustomed to working so hard and giving the poor such considerate attention.
3. In order to be of use to others in the city of Poitiers, rather than just those under his immediate care, Father Grignion assumed the additional duties of preaching in various churches, hearing confessions, visiting the needy, and teaching catechism to young and old alike.

Chapters 5 through 8—In Which Father de Montfort Returns and Begins to Preach True Devotion to the Blessed Virgin Mary

1. The Wisdom Group, as established by Father Grignion, was "a number of women invalids at the poorhouse who were leading something of the religious life" (page 27). Those who were able helped Father Grignion with his various duties. All members prayed, especially to our Lady. The name of the group derived from the fact that the cross—suffering—is wisdom. Their sufferings were offered for sinners throughout the world.
2. Father Grignion assumed the name "Father de Montfort," relinquishing his family name (surname) in the spirit of holy poverty. Perhaps this was in response to Jesus' call to holy poverty in imitation of Him as indicated in Matthew 8:20 and elsewhere.
3. Under Father de Montfort's guidance, Mary Louise prepared for over four weeks before formally making the Act of Consecration to our Lady. During this time of preparation, she studied the Gospel of Matthew, read selected passages from *The Imitation of Christ*, and prayed specific formal prayers in order to help her renounce the world as well as increase her knowledge of herself, the Blessed Virgin, and Jesus Christ.

Chapters 9 through 12—In Which Father de Montfort Founds the Daughters of Wisdom

1. When Mary Louise's parents were asked to give their permission for Mary Louise to join Father de Montfort at the poorhouse, Mary Louise's father John was secretly pleased with his daughter's decision and gave his permission readily. Her mother burst into tears, worried about what other people would think. Mary Louise stated that she wanted to take this step as Father de Montfort, her spiritual director who takes the place of Christ on earth, had suggested it, indicating that it was God's Will for her.
2. Mary Louise's "Baptism" for her new dress occurred when Father de Montfort asked her to walk through the town of Poiters—especially up and down the main street—so everyone could see her new habit. This was truly an act of obedience and humility.

Chapters 13 through 15—In Which Father de Montfort Leaves, Returns, and Again Leaves Poitiers

1. Since his early days in the seminary, Father de Montfort's secret ambition had been to become a missionary priest in the New World. Now he felt drawn to preach missions and retreats in France and to teach catechism. He hoped to form a little company of priests to help him.
2. In his search for God's Will, Father de Montfort went to a poorhouse in Paris where he was criticized and misunderstood as chaplain. When he was dismissed there, he obtained a room under the stairway of a dilapidated house. Several weeks later the bishop offered to take him

to Cardinal de Noailles, who sent Father de Montfort to live with the hermits of Mont Valérien work with them on keeping the rule. Thereafter, he returned to his room under the stairs to pray until a letter arrived requesting that he return to the poorhouse in Pointers, which he did.

3. Father de Montfort gained the respect of the hermits of Mont Valérien by acting as peacemaker—listening patiently to every complaint, putting himself in the place of each one who came to him. Then he would point out that the best thing to do was to turn to the Blessed Virgin for guidance, teaching the hermits that our Lady was their best friend and a source of true peace.

Chapters 16 through 19—In Which Father de Montfort Begins His Street Preaching in Earnest and Incurs the Wrath of the Jansenists

1. Father de Montfort believed the easiest way to know, love, and serve God is with the help of the Blessed Virgin.
2. When giving missions and wresting souls from the hands of the devil, Father de Montfort won God's blessing on his work by mortifying himself with penance. He believed that only suffering won the grace needed for the defeat of the devil.

Chapters 20 through 23—In Which Pope Clement XI Blesses Father de Montfort's Vocation of Preaching, Prayer, and Suffering

1. Father de Montfort traveled to Rome to discuss his vocation to the foreign missions with Pope Clement XI. Father de Montfort half-expected the Holy Father to turn down his request. Pope Clement XI stated that Father de Montfort was to return to France as his vocation was to preach, pray, and suffer in his battle against the Jansenists.
2. Upon Father de Montfort's return from Rome, the bishop of Poiters told Father de Montfort that he was not only forbidden to preach in the Diocese of Poiters but also to offer Mass in any church or chapel. He was also ordered to leave the city within twenty-four hours.

Chapters 24 through 27—In Which Father de Montfort's Preaching And Example Convert Many People, but He Still Continues to Make Enemies

1. The Blessed Virgin promised Blessed Alan that those who say the rosary devoutly would be rewarded in four specific ways: They will receive special protection and very great graces, they will not be overwhelmed by misfortune or die a bad death, they will be delivered promptly from Purgatory, and they will obtain what they ask through the rosary (page 125).
2. The habit of both Dominican brothers and priests is white. Additionally the priests wear a white scapular over their tunic, while the brothers wear a black scapular.
3. The two-hundred-year-old legend of the prophecy of St. Vincent Ferrer regarding the chapel of Our Lady of Pity was that someone not yet born in St. Vincent's time would restore and complete the project. This man would be unknown in the region—someone who would be laughed at and contradicted (page 133).
4. Father de Montfort was asked to leave Brittany as he had disobeyed Father Ledeuger by requesting alms during a retreat or mission. Father de Montfort intended that the money be used for Masses to be offered for the Holy Souls in Purgatory, but it was a violation of the rules.

Chapters 28 through 31—In Which Father de Montfort and His Companions Continue to Be Misunderstood and Their Virtue Tested

1. The "new companion" acquired by Father de Montfort and Brother Mathurin after leaving Brittany was Brother John, a young man who wished to join Father in making our Lady better known to others. (In 1710 another brother, Brother Nicholas, also joined Father de Montfort.)
2. Father de Montfort and his companions went to Nantes after the bishop of Saint-Malo forbid Father to preach or hear confessions at the Chapel of Our Lady of Wisdom. Father felt there was work for them in Nantes.

3. In answer to his prayer for guidance on the building site of the Calvary shrine, two white doves appeared carrying off earth from the excavation site. When they were followed, a mound of earth marked the new building site upon the top of a beautiful hill with an impressive view.
4. After the bishop had the Calvary destroyed and revoked his permission for Father de Montfort to preach and hear confessions in the Nantes diocese, Father de Montfort decided to become a tertiary member of the Dominican order. (The Calvary of Pontchâteau was rebuilt in 1821. If desired, search online for more information.)

Chapters 32 through 35—In Which Father de Montfort Battles the Calvinists and Works to Build His Dream of the Company of Mary

1. Although the influence of Jansenism was less widespread in the dioceses of Lucon and LaRochelle, Father de Montfort and his band of brothers still had enemies in the Calvinists.
2. The four brothers in the company of Father de Montfort around 1712 included Brothers Mathurin, John, Nicholas, and Gabriel.
3. Father de Montfort went to Paris in August of 1713 searching for candidates for the Company of Mary. On his return trip, he planned to stop in Poiters to see Sister Mary Louise for their first visit in over eight years.

Chapters 36 through 39—In Which Sister Mary Louise Moves to La Rochelle, the Company of Mary Grows, and Father Louis de Montfort Dies

1. Father de Montfort surprised Sister Mary Louise by visiting her in Poiters; they had not seen each other in over eight years. Additionally, he shared with her his plan to open a free school for girls in La Rochelle. He wanted her to move to La Rochelle to help teach.
2. Father René Mulot, a frail young priest paralyzed on one side, agreed to join the Company of Mary; Father de Montfort assured him that if he did, all his ills would vanish.
3. As his life's work, Father de Montfort felt he had "a few writings, his missions, the Daughters of Wisdom with four members, and the Company of Mary with seven brothers and two priests. . . . And I wanted to do so much!" (pages 197-198).
4. The reported last words of Father Louis de Montfort were "I am all Thine, and all I have is Thine, O most loving Jesus, through Mary, Thy holy Mother" (page 200).

Epilogue—In Which the Company of Mary and the Daughters of Wisdom Carry on the Work of Father Louis de Montfort

1. The pastor of Loges told the parishioners that Father Mulot and Father Vatel would stay for an additional week and give a mission for the entire countryside. As he suspected when he planned this little trick, the priests reluctantly followed through. The mission was a great success, and Father Mulot and Fr Vatel gained confidence in their abilities to preach.
2. By 1940, the Company of Mary and the Daughters of Wisdom had expanded into Haiti, Canada, Holland, Columbia, Denmark, United States, British Columbia, Iceland, East Africa, Madagascar, the Belgian Congo, Borneo, Belgium, Italy, and England.

Answer Key to Book Summary Test

1. At a time in history where many people believed that religion should not make people happy and no attention should be given to the Blessed Virgin and the saints (They should not be too familiar and lovable.), St. Louis de Montfort preached sermons about devotion to the Blessed Virgin as the easiest way to know, love, and serve God. He believed in the power of the rosary. He taught that devotion to Mary is a simple, humble way of attaining holiness. Many people misunderstood his term "slaves of Jesus through Mary."
2. Throughout his life in the various dioceses in which he preached, St. Louis de Montfort battled both the Jansenists and the Calvinists.

3. St. Louis de Montfort believed that we should make an Act of Consecration to our Lady giving her everything—ourselves, our possessions, and the satisfactory merit of our prayers and works. He quoted St. Bernard, "If you wish to present something to God no matter how small it may be, place it in Mary's hands if you do not wish to be refused" (pages 167-68). The short form of the Act of Consecration is to be recited each morning: "I am all Thine and all that I have is Thine, O most loving Jesus, through Mary, Thy holy Mother." He promoted the daily recitation of the rosary while meditating on its mysteries. He used the word "slave" to indicate our relationship to Jesus through Mary.

4. St. Louis de Montfort's accomplishments include his writings—*True Devotion to the Blessed Virgin,* and *Letter to the Friends of the Cross*—the religious Rules he wrote for the Company of Mary and the Daughters of Wisdom, and many original hymns (164 of which have been preserved). He also established two religious orders, The Company of Mary and The Daughters of Wisdom. He left us the doctrine of True Devotion to Mary as well as his example of obedience, humilty, love of suffering, and a thirst for bringing souls to Jesus through Mary. He converted many sinners and brought countless souls back from the errors of Jansenism. (St. Louis also wrote two books not mentioned in this biography: *The Secret of the Rosary,* which was published after his death, and *Love of Eternal Wisdom.*)

5. Answers will vary.

Other RACE for Heaven Products

Catholic Study Guides for Mary Fabyan Windeatt's Saint Biography Series teach the Catholic faith to all members of your family. Written with your family's various learning levels in mind, these flexible study guides succeed as stand-alone unit studies or supplements to your regular curriculum. Thirty to sixty minutes per day will allow your family to experience:

- ☑ The spirituality and holy habits of the saints
- ☑ Lively family discussions on important faith topics
- ☑ Increased critical thinking and reading comprehension skills
- ☑ Quality read-aloud time with Catholic "living books"
- ☑ Enhanced knowledge of Catholic doctrine and the Bible
- ☑ History and geography incorporated into saintly literature
- ☑ Writing projects based on secular and Catholic historical events and characters

Purchase these guides individually or in the following grade-level packages. (Grade level is are determined solely on the length of each book in the series.)

Grades 3-4: *St. Thomas Aquinas, The Story of the "Dumb Ox"*; *St. Catherine of Siena, The Girl Who Saw Saints in the Sky*; *Patron Saint of First Communicants, The Story of Blessed Imelda Lambertini*; and *The Miraculous Medal, The Story of Our Lady's Appearances to St. Catherine Labouré*

Grade 5: *St. Rose, First Canonized Saint of the Americas*; *St. Martin de Porres, The Story of the Little Doctor of Lima, Peru*; *King David and His Songs, A Story of the Psalms*; and *Blessed Marie of New France, The Story of the First Missionary Sisters in Canada*

Grade 6: *St. Dominic, Preacher of the Rosary and Founder of the Dominicans*; *St. Benedict, The Story of the Father of the Western Monks*; *The Children of Fatima and Our Lady's Message to the World*; and *St. John Masias, Marvelous Dominican Gate-keeper of Lima, Peru*

Grade 7: *The Little Flower, The Story of St. Therese of the Child Jesus*; *St. Hyacinth, The Story of the Apostle of the North*; *The Curé of Ars, The Story of St. John Vianney, Patron Saint of Parish Priests*; and *St. Louis de Montfort, The Story of Our Lady's Slave*

Grade 8: *Pauline Jaricot, Foundress of the Living Rosary and the Society for the Propagation of Faith*; *St. Francis Solano, Wonder-Worker of the New World and Apostle of Argentina and Peru*; *St. Paul the Apostle, The Story of the Apostle to the Gentiles*; and *St. Margaret Mary, Apostle of the Sacred Heart*

The Windeatt Dictionary: Pre-Vatican II Terms and Catholic Words from Mary Fabyan Windeatt's Saint Biographies explains over 450 Catholic terms and expressions used in this popular saint biography series. Indispensable in expanding knowledge and practice of the Catholic faith, this book provides a ready access for the Catholic vocabulary words used in the RACE for Heaven Windeatt study guides. This dictionary also includes a Catholic book report resource that contains suggestions for forty-five Catholic book reports: fourteen writing projects, ten book report activities, and twenty-one topics for saint biographies.

Graced Encounters with Mary Fabyan Windeatt's Saints: 344 Ways to Imitate the Holy Habits of the Saints is a compilation of the "Growing in Holiness" sections of RACE for Heaven's Catholic study guides for the Windeatt saint biography series and presents 344 examples of saintly behavior, one for nearly every chapter in each of these twenty biographies. Enhance your encounter with the saints by practicing the models of devotion, service, penance, prayer, and virtue offered in this guide.

Bedtime Bible Stories for Catholic Children: Loving Jesus through His Word contains twenty discussions of Bible stories that were originally published in serial form in a Catholic children's magazine. Their author stated, "The tales are extremely simple and unadorned. They are real conversations of a real child and her mother." Due to popular demand, the series was later (1910) published as a book, *Bible Stories Told to "Toddles."* The engaging conversational style of this book lends itself well as a bedtime read-aloud that allows Jesus to come alive in the Gospels. The study aids include discussion questions to help foster spiritual conversation, Bible excerpts relevant to the presented story, "Growing in Holiness" suggestions for living the Gospel message in our daily lives, and short catechism lessons for both children and adults.

I Talk with God: The Art of Prayer and Meditation for Catholic Children strives to instill in young Catholics a love of prayer and a practical knowledge of the art of meditation. This prayer book contains prayers to pray out loud (vocal prayer) or in the silence of your heart. It shows how you can talk with God, and more importantly, how you can love God. As you progress through this book—from discovering what prayer is to reading and reciting simple prayers to understanding meditation and then to helps for deeper meditation—you will see that prayer and meditation often go together. Meditation is described by the big *Catechism of the Catholic Church* as nothing more than "prayerful reflection" or *holy thinking.* You can use books, devotions, pictures, holy cards, and images (such as the stained glass windows in church) to help you think about holy people, events, and ideas. Learn how to talk with God each day to increase your love for Him and follow more closely His holy will.

Communion with the Saints: A Family Preparation Program for First Communion and Beyond in the Spirit of St. Therese imitates St. Therese of the Child Jesus and her family who studied and prayed for sixty-nine days in anticipation of Therese's First Holy Communion. Modeling this preparation, the *Communion with the Saints* program will help any family find renewed fervor in the reception of the Eucharist. This resource includes a chapter-by-chapter study of the following four books:

- *The Little Flower, The Story of Saint Therese of the Child Jesus*—to provide the foundation of God's love for us and to encourage a desire for holiness

- *The Children of Fatima and Our Lady's Message to the World*—to show the sinfulness of our world and the need to avoid sin

- *The Patron Saint of First Communicants, The Story of Blessed Imelda Lambertini*—to inspire devotion to the Sacrament of Holy Communion

- *The King of the Golden City* by Mother Mary Loyola —to illustrate Jesus' Presence as a source of grace necessary to live a holy life

Each of the sixty-nine days of preparation includes read-aloud selections with enrichment activities, meditational readings, catechism lessons, and plenty of practical application to promote a growth in holiness and sanctity. Weekend suggestions include a list of over thirty-five family projects. The use of *My First Communion Journal* is encouraged with this program.

My First Communion Journal in Imitation of Saint Therese, The Little Flower provides a lasting keepsake of a child's First Holy Communion. This journal has been constructed in imitation of the copybook made for Therese Martin by her older sister Pauline to help Therese prepare for her First Holy Communion. Although this book is not an exact replica of the copybook used by Therese, it does contain many of the same prayers and aspirations she used, the same idea of flowers inspiring virtue, and the same method of recording prayers recited and sacrifices made. It is up to you to decorate and complete this journal, replicating Therese's heroic efforts by raising your mind and heart to Jesus and by humbling yourself with small sacrifices. Learn as well to imitate St. Therese's love and knowledge of Scripture as you meditate on—or even memorize—the biblical passages that are provided for reflection. This journal may be completed in conjunction with the *Communion with the Saints* program or used separately.

My First Communion Journal in Imitation of St. Paul, Putting on the Armor of God was also inspired by St. Therese's copybook and uses the same method of encouraging—and recording—daily prayers and mortifications. However, instead of using flowers to illustrate virtues, this resource uses the battle model St. Paul describes in Ephesians 6:10-17. First communicants are encouraged to arm themselves with virtues and spiritual weapons in order to fight as soldiers of Christ. The scriptural words of Jesus and St. Paul are reflected on frequently to encourage the imitation of the actions and love of Jesus and to inspire a love and knowledge of Holy Scripture. This journal too may be completed in conjunction with the *Communion with the Saints* program or used separately.

The King of the Golden City Study Edition is a new edition of a book that was originally published in 1921. This treasure of a book was written in response to a student's appeal for instructions along with "little stories" to help her prepare for Holy Communion. To fulfill this request, Mother Loyola of the Bar Convent in York, England, wrote a simple story that illustrates Jesus' desire to share an intimate relationship with each one of His children. This new edition contains some updated language but, quite deliberately, does not contain any pictures. Readers, as they progress through this story, will form a mental image of their King, one as unique and personal as their own relationship with Him. The study sections assist with the allegory, connect to the Bible as well as to the catechism, and explore the art of prayer in the spirit of the three Carmelite Doctors of the Church. Although written over ninety years ago for a young child, this book remains a timeless masterpiece of Catholic literature suitable for all ages. (Also available as a study guide only)

The Good Shepherd and His Little Lambs Study Edition is a simply told Catholic tale of four children who meet with their beloved aunt for "First Communion talks." More than a story, it is a First Communion primer that takes the tenets of the catechism and, through naturally-flowing conversations, relates them in the language of little ones to authentic Christian living. As Mrs. Bosch explains, "We might learn the catechism all the way through beautifully, and at the end find ourselves still very stiff and clumsy about loving our Lord. When He comes to us, we don't want to welcome Him into our souls only with answers out of the catechism, do we?" Enriched by appropriate Biblical passages, points of doctrine, and prayers, this story-primer is an enjoyable and effective read-aloud that will prepare the Good Shepherd's little lambs to worthily receive Him in the Holy Eucharist.

A Reconciliation Reader-Retreat: Read-Aloud Lessons, Stories, and Poems for Young Catholics Preparing for Confession provides a basic doctrinal explanation and review of the Sacrament of Reconciliation as well as a Gospel examination of conscience—a seven-day read-aloud formation retreat. To help the lessons come alive and to enable young Catholics to more readily apply these doctrines to their own daily lives, the lessons have been supplemented with pertinent short stories and poems. Each lesson contains reflection questions, a family prayer, and a "Gospel Examination of Conscience" that is formulated according to the dictates of the *Catechism of the Catholic Church*. This reader-retreat will not only enrich and deepen the sacramental experience for each member of your family but it will also provide several tools to help you recommit to leading a virtuous life and to grow together in holiness.

Devotion to St. Joseph: Read-Aloud Stories, Poems, and Prayers for Catholic Children encourages children to love Jesus as St. Joseph did. As Scripture does not record a single word this great saint spoke; we must take our lessons of his life from his actions. In this compilation of stories and poems about our Savior's foster-father from renowned Catholics, children of all ages are encouraged to imitate the virtues the life of St. Joseph reveal to us in his loving dedication to Jesus and Mary. The discussion questions as well as the reflections on the virtues of St. Joseph lead children to apply the lessons of this saint's life to their own while the prayer section promotes a lasting devotion to the great St. Joseph. As St. Teresa of Avila declared, "I wish I could persuade everyone to be devoted to this glorious saint!"

The Month of St. Joseph: Prayers and Practices for Each Day of March in Imitation of the Virtues of St. Joseph was originally published in 1874. This book contains daily meditations on the life and virtues of St. Joseph for adults and high-school students. In addition, each day presents a prayer to St. Joseph, several resolutions, a short ejaculatory prayer, a relevant Scripture verse, and a brief consideration for reflection. The practices for each day are intended to assist the reader in acquiring the habits of prayer and interior recollection so necessary to living in the presence of God. Perfect for Lenten reading, this journey through the life of St. Joseph reveals his love of God and neighbor, humility, quiet action, and spirit of sacrifice. While the Bible tells so little about St. Joseph's life, here we discover the abundant virtues of this silent saint—and are challenged to imitate them.

Alternative Book Reports for Catholic Students contains forty-five book report ideas to encourage critical thinking for ages seven to fourteen. These ideas are intended to provoke a reflection on those themes and topics that support and encourage Catholic living as well as some that may conflict with our Faith. Many report topics require an examination of our personal faith life and prompt us to take lessons from the saints to strengthen our own faith in God. The suggested activities vary from written exercises to creative art projects and include twenty-one topics specifically designed for saint biographies. Other activities can be used within a group or family.

Reading the Saints: Lists of Catholic Books for Children Plus Book Collecting Tips for the Home and School Library (formerly entitled *Saintly Resources*) is a valuable tool for Catholic home educators, classroom teachers, and collectors of Catholic juvenile books. This resource will help you discover living books from such popular out-of-print Catholic juvenile series as Catholic Treasury, Vision Books, and American Background Books as well as current series books for young Catholics. Use this book to find:

- Over 800 Catholic books listed by author, series, reading level, century, and geographical location
- More than 275 authors of saint biographies, historical fiction, and poetry written for Catholic juvenile readers
- Publishers of Catholic children's books, present and past
- Helpful advice for collecting and caring for used books
- Hundreds of age-appropriate, accessible living books to enrich your study of the Catholic Church's rich heritage of saints and notable Catholic historical figures
- Information on how to build and maintain your own library of Catholic juvenile books
- Inspiring quotations about book collecting, reading, and the love of books

The Outlaws of Ravenhurst Study Edition contains a classic story of the persecution of Scottish Catholics that was first written in 1923 and was revised and reprinted in 1950. This 2009 edition of Sr. M. Imelda Wallace's *Outlaws of Ravenhurst* contains the revised story of 1950 plus chapter-by-chapter aids to assist readers in assimilating the book's strong Catholic elements into their own lives. The study section focuses on critical thinking, integration of biblical teachings, and the study of the virtuous life to which Christ calls us as mature Catholics. With its emphasis on virtues (theological and moral plus the gifts and fruits of the Holy Spirit), the spiritual and corporal works of mercy, and the Beatitudes, *Outlaws of Ravenhurst Study Edition* is a fun and effective catechetical tool for Catholics preparing for the Sacrament of Confirmation. (Also available as a study guide only)

The Family that Overtook Christ Study Edition: The Story of the Family of St. Bernard of Clairvaux is an excellent read for young adults who are preparing to receive the Sacrament of Confirmation. In this exciting chronicle of the life of twelfth-century knights, we have an entire family of nine saints who lay before us their individual means of achieving intimate union with Christ. Learn with the Fontaines family how to supernaturalize the natural, develop a God-consciousness, and attain sanctity by being yourself. Perfect for high-school read-aloud (or adult study), this new study edition has over 250 footnotes for increased comprehension and provides discussion/meditation points to promote the art of spiritual conversation. The appendix lists formulas of Catholic doctrine that are essential for confirmands not only to know but also to incorporate into their own spiritual lives.

A Confirmation Reader-Retreat: Read-Aloud Lessons, Stories and Poems for Young Catholics utilizes chapters from two excellent out-of-print Catholic books for children (*I Belong to God, Great Truths in Simple Stories for Children and Lovers of Children* by Lillian Clark; and *Children's Retreats in Preparation for First Confession, First Holy Communion, and Confirmation* by Rev. P.A. Halpin). This book provides a basic doctrinal review of the Sacrament of Confirmation as well as prayer experiences—a nine-day read-aloud retreat/novena. The reprinted material has been supplemented with short stories and poems that provide insights in applying catechetical doctrines to the daily life of young Catholics. Each lesson concludes with "I Talk with God"—a section that encourages readers (of all ages) to deepen their relationship with each of the Three Persons of the Blessed Trinity. Reflection questions promote the habit of spiritual conversation within your family—to encourage family members to discuss holy topics—and to help you grow together in holiness. Additionally, a traditional novena to the Holy Spirit is included.

By Cross and Anchor Study Edition: The Story of Frederic Baraga on Lake Superior relates the exciting, and often miraculous, missionary adventures of the "Snowshoe Priest"—Venerable Frederic Baraga, the first bishop of Michigan's Upper Peninsula. Declared "Venerable" by Pope Benedict XVI on May 10, 2012, this priest came to the United States from Slovenia in 1830 to undertake his mission as a "simple servant of God." For almost forty years, Fr. Frederic Baraga traveled across over 80,000 square miles of wilderness by snowshoe in winter and canoe in summer. In imitation of Christ, Bishop Baraga become poor so that he might bring the riches of the Catholic Faith to the Chippewa and immigrant residents of the beautiful peninsula he served. Although not strictly a biography, this book is a story based on historical facts drawn from Bishop Baraga's own journal and letters—a fascinating, easy-to-read history of Michigan's northern peninsula. While this exciting adventure is intended for youth who are interested in knowing more about this quiet, courageous priest, readers of all ages will be inspired by his life of humility, simplicity, and selfless virtue. This new study edition contains over 130 footnotes, defining less familiar vocabulary words and—gleaned from Venerable Baraga's *Journal* and other primary sources—details regarding the region's people and places. Also included are discussion questions, applicable Scripture passages, pertinent quotations of Venerable Baraga from the text, and—most importantly—a section illustrating how to imitate the various virtues of Venerable Frederic Baraga. Additionally, the complete text of Bishop Baraga's 1853 "Pastoral Letter to the Faithful" has been included with numerous references added in order that we may read this in light of Scripture and the *Compendium of the Catechism of the Catholic Church*. Learn more about the life, ministry, and heroic virtues of Venerable Frederic Baraga, the "Snowshoe Priest."

To Order: Email info@RACEforHeaven.com or place an order at RACEforHeaven.com. Discover, MasterCard, VISA, PayPal, American Express, checks, and money orders are accepted.

www.ingramcontent.com/pod-product-compliance
Lightning Source LLC
Chambersburg PA
CBHW081105270725
30205CB00036B/524